Contributing Editor
Gisela Lee

Editorial Project Manager
Karen J. Goldfluss, M.S. Ed.

Editor in Chief
Sharon Coan, M.S. Ed.

Illustrator
Victoria Ponikvar Frazier
Larry Bauer

Cover Artist
Denise Bauer

Art Coordinator
Cheri Macoubrie Wilson

Creative Director
Elayne Roberts

Imaging
Ralph Olmedo, Jr.

Product Manager
Phil Garcia

Publishers:
Rachelle Cracchiolo, M.S. Ed.
Mary Dupuy Smith, M.S. Ed.

Jumbo Teacher Tips and Timesavers

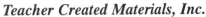

Getting Ready for School

Educational Techniques

Communicators

Behavior Management

Classroom Environment

and more

Authors

Denise Dodds Harrell, Barbara Hillis, Julia Jasmine, and Dona Herweck Rice

Teacher Created Materials

Teacher Created Materials, Inc.
6421 Industry Way
Westminster, CA 92683
www.teachercreated.com

©1999 Teacher Created Materials, Inc.
Reprinted, 2000
Made in U.S.A.
ISBN-1-57690-314-1

Table of Contents

Table of Contents *(cont.)*

Introduction

Congratulations! You are a teacher! You have learned the ins and outs of child psychology, effective classroom management, curriculum development, and even how to operate an overhead projector—but now what? Now you are in the classroom, on your own, and all that wonderful training may not seem like quite enough to get you through the real world of teaching. Rest assured, your teacher training is excellent groundwork for the path ahead; however, your real training is about to begin—in the classroom.

Virtually everything you will need to make your first year a smooth and comfortable one can be found in the pages of this book. Written and compiled by veteran teachers, the book contains tried-and-true tips, forms, and plans for every first-year teacher. You will find the following:

- **classroom management forms**

- **management and discipline techniques**

- **suggestions for whole-class, independent, and cooperative learning**

- **assessment tips and forms**

- **how to keep and use portfolios**

- **behavior management ideas**

- **parent and student communicators**

- **tips for volunteer management**

- **how to use a substitute effectively**

- **cross-curricular work sheets and activities**

- **resources**

Of course, even an experienced teacher will find a great deal of support and new ideas in the following pages. It is never too late to learn something new!

When all is said and done, learning how to operate the overhead is one thing, but knowing when to use it and who to rely upon for help is even more useful. With the supporting ideas here, you will have the time and energy to put all your classroom training to effective and positive use.

Good luck and best wishes as you embark on this exciting and rewarding new career!

Student Supplies

While all public schools are required to provide necessary supplies for students, it may prove helpful if your students keep a box or bag of some basic supplies themselves. You can request that parents send these, being sure to let them know that they are not required to do so. You might also ask parents to send additional supplies for those students without means. It never hurts to ask local stationery and other supply stores for donations to your classroom stock. You may get negative responses, but the only way to get a positive one is to ask.

Here is a wish list of supplies that will prove useful for each student to have in his or her possession.

- scissors
- glue stick
- white glue
- box of crayons
- set of colored marking pens or pencils
- pencils

- eraser
- pens (for upper grades)
- ruler
- tissue paper
- folder
- spiral assignment pad

Teacher Supplies

There are many things you will find useful to have at the ready in your classroom. Hopefully, your school is well supplied and able to provide you with everything you need. However, that is not always the case.

In a perfect world, you will be supplied with each of the following to begin your year. If not, acquire what you can. Do not be afraid to ask for donations! Everything goes much smoother with the right supplies.

- lined writing paper (appropriate to grade level)
- blank drawing paper
- colored construction paper
- file folders
- envelopes
- pencils
- crayons
- markers
- permanent markers
- colored pencils
- scissors
- glue sticks
- white glue
- yard or meter stick

- paper clips
- rubber bands
- masking tape
- clear tape
- stapler
- staples
- pushpins
- safety pins
- brads
- hole punch
- three-hole punch
- pencil sharpener
- chalk or dry-erase pens
- pointer
- textbooks
- literature books

- overhead transparencies, Thermo-Fax masters, and/or ditto paper
- overhead projector
- easel
- easel chart or tablet
- projection screen
- cassette or compact disc player
- computer and printer
- chalkboard or dry-erase board
- rulers

Don't Throw It Away!

Teachers have developed a reputation over the years for being the world's biggest pack rats. This is due to the simple fact that teachers can immediately see the intrinsic worth of everything!

Here is a list of items that many people may throw away but that you are likely to find abundantly useful at some point throughout the year. It just goes to show you, one man's trash is another man's treasure!

- plastic film containers
- foam meat trays
- plastic strawberry baskets
- plastic tomato baskets
- old magazines
- used wrapping paper
- old newspapers
- used greeting and holiday cards
- Styrofoam packing peanuts
- large cardboard boxes
- plastic cups (the printed kind for children from some movie theaters and restaurants)
- junk mail advertisements
- rubber bands

- plastic tabs from loaves of bread
- twist ties
- metal bandage containers
- plastic pantyhose eggs
- egg cartons
- plastic milk cartons
- old calendars
- scraps of colored paper
- free stickers (from the dentist, grocer, junk mail, etc.)
- cottage cheese, yogurt, and sour cream tubs
- old, clean socks
- old, adult-sized shirts

Goals, Objectives, and Unit Plans

The most important thing to do as a teacher is to organize your goals, objectives, and unit plans. Formulating goals and objectives is a major part of a teacher's course of study, but they are only the beginning. The key is to take them and to give them real-world applications. These come in the form of your day-to-day lessons.

The chart below can serve as a mini-refresher course on the purpose and flow of goals and objectives. The next page will outline the basic steps involved in formulating a lesson. The forms that follow can be used to develop and to organize your plans. Remember, everything you do to prepare will be well worth it when the school day begins.

The goal may cover a period of weeks or months.

Sample Goal: Students will learn about plants.

The long-range objective may cover a period of one to three weeks.

Sample Long-Range Objective: Students will understand the various parts of plants and their functions.

The instructional objective may cover a single day's lesson.

Sample Instructional Objective: Students will list various parts of a flower.

Lesson Design

This lesson plan works for individual lessons as well as for lessons that may require several days to complete. Remember that if a lesson continues for more than one day, students will need to be refocused on the objective of the lesson, and the teacher will need to check that the students remember what they have learned or worked on before continuing.

Set: Get the students ready to learn.

Objective:

Purpose of the lesson:

Instruction: Learning may be broken down into several parts.

Input:

Model:

Check understanding:

Guided Practice: Practice the new learning with the teacher.

Activity:

Materials or supplies:

Closure: Make the connection and final check for understanding with the students between the learning and the guided practice activity.

Independent Practice: Check to be sure that the practice or activity relates to the objective of the lesson.

Activity:

Materials or supplies:

Brainstorm Forms for Unit Activities

Duplicate the forms on pages 10–15 as needed when preparing your plans.

Goal:

Long-Range Objectives:

Unit Topic:

Teacher Read-Alouds	**Student Reading**

Brainstorm Forms for
Unit Activities *(cont.)*

Language Arts	**Science**

Social Studies	**Math**

Brainstorm Forms for
Unit Activities *(cont.)*

Physical Education/Movement	Art

Music	Culminating Activity

Planning Web

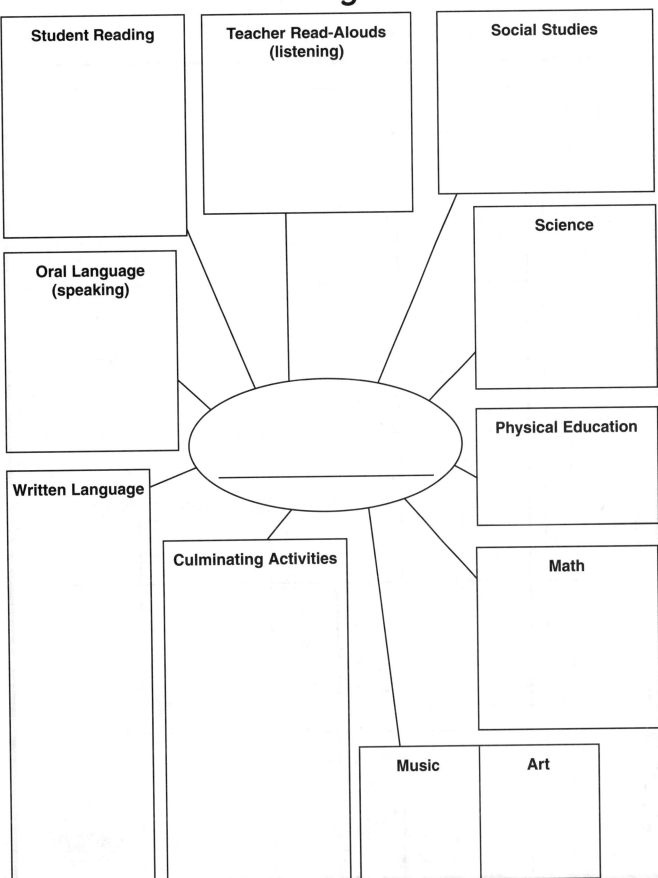

Student Reading

Teacher Read-Alouds (listening)

Social Studies

Oral Language (speaking)

Science

Physical Education

Written Language

Culminating Activities

Math

Music

Art

Unit Planning Form

Duplicate, punch holes, and insert into a binder.

Unit: _____					
Week of: _____					
Monday					
Tuesday					
Wednesday					
Thursday					
Friday					

Unit Planning Form (cont.)

Notes:				

Teacher Note: Here and on the next three pages are activities that are useful during the first day or week of school.

Getting to Know You

Directions: Walk around the room and talk to your new classmates. Find someone to match each group of words below. Write that person's name on the blank line. You may use a person's name only once. You may also use your own name but only once as well.

Find someone who . . .

1. has a pet_____

2. enjoys singing_____

3. can play a musical instrument _____

4. knows karate _____

5. likes to use a computer _____

6. is able to swim _____

7. enjoys reading books _____

8. was born in a foreign country_____

9. wears contact lenses _____

10. has an older brother_____

11. has a younger sister_____

12. likes to eat yogurt_____

13. has hit a home run _____

14. has read a *Clifford the Big Red Dog* book _____

15. can make a basket from the free-throw line_____

Sharing Thoughts and Feelings

Directions: Write an ending for each of these sentence starters. Team up with a partner to read and talk about each other's sentences.

1. I am happiest when _____

2. I would like to learn to _____

3. My favorite food is _____

4. The food I dislike most is _____

5. When I wake up in the morning, I usually feel _____

6. I like people who _____

7. Something that scares me is _____

8. I would like to be better at _____

9. When I am worried about something, I usually _____

10. Life seems great when _____

Write and Draw

Part I.

Directions: Read each of the following sentence starters and then write endings.

1. I will always remember _____

   _____

2. A book I would like to read again is _____

   _____

3. If a person is really your friend, _____

   _____

4. My favorite sport is _____

   _____

5. If I could go anyplace in the world, _____

   _____

Part II.

Directions: Now choose one of the five sentences above and use it as a topic sentence for a complete paragraph. Think about your ideas before you write the paragraph.

_____

_____

_____

_____

_____

_____

_____

_____

_____

_____

_____

Write and Draw *(cont.)*

Part III.

Directions: Draw a picture about the paragraph you wrote. When you finish, share your sentences, paragraph, and picture in a small group.

Bulletin Boards

It is always a good idea to have interesting bulletin boards and displays around your room. These can satisfy a variety of needs, including the presentation of student work, the imparting of important information, and the reinforcement of key elements in the curriculum.

Classroom Information Bulletin Board

Choose a bulletin board somewhere conspicuous in your classroom. Post important classroom management information. This information is helpful in establishing routines for children, parents, and other visitors. It is also vital information for substitute teachers.

Suggested information for the bulletin board includes the following:

- emergency information including evacuation route
- location of substitute folder
- daily schedule
- bell schedule
- lunch and rainy day lunch schedule
- class lists (without addresses and telephone numbers as these are sometimes confidential)
- class rules or expectations
- times that students leave the room for special services, such as assemblies.

Featured Author/Artist Bulletin Board

Featuring an author or illustrator in an area of your classroom is very motivating for the students. It allows students to enjoy the talents of creative people. This type of bulletin board teaches students to appreciate the different styles of authors and artists.

Some suggestions for this bulletin board include the following:

- name of author or artist
- facts about the person
- interest baskets with the featured author or artist's works (Keep these interest baskets in the reading corner upon completion of featuring this author/artist. Children will enjoy going back to familiar works and will be on the lookout for more to add to the collection.)
- book jackets or prints of works
- cassette tapes to accompany author's work
- duplicated copies or pages from an author/artist's work and tracing paper (The children will trace and very closely recreate a particular drawing using various art media found in the art area.)
- a graph or tally sheet for students' critiques of a book (Give two choices from which students will choose. Select, for example: Which book do you like better? Which character would you like to be?, or Is this book reality or fantasy?)

Teacher Note: Use these calendars for the classroom wall, for your record planning, or in students' notebooks for their own records.

September

Sunday	Monday	Tuesday	Wednesday	Thursday	Friday	Saturday

October

Sunday	Monday	Tuesday	Wednesday	Thursday	Friday	Saturday

November

	Sunday	Monday	Tuesday	Wednesday	Thursday	Friday	Saturday

December

Sunday	Monday	Tuesday	Wednesday	Thursday	Friday	Saturday

January

Sunday	Monday	Tuesday	Wednesday	Thursday	Friday	Saturday

February

Sunday	Monday	Tuesday	Wednesday	Thursday	Friday	Saturday

March

Sunday	Monday	Tuesday	Wednesday	Thursday	Friday	Saturday

April

Sunday	Monday	Tuesday	Wednesday	Thursday	Friday	Saturday

May

	Sunday	Monday	Tuesday	Wednesday	Thursday	Friday	Saturday

June

Sunday	Monday	Tuesday	Wednesday	Thursday	Friday	Saturday

July

Sunday	Monday	Tuesday	Wednesday	Thursday	Friday	Saturday

August

	Sunday	Monday	Tuesday	Wednesday	Thursday	Friday	Saturday

Things to Do This Week

Monday:

Tuesday:

Wednesday:

Thursday:

Friday:

Weekend:

THINGS THAT NEED TO BE DONE

❑ _____

❑ _____

❑ _____

❑ _____

❑ _____

❑ _____

❑ _____

❑ _____

❑ _____

❑ _____

❑ _____

❑ _____

❑ _____

❑ _____

❑ _____

❑ _____

❑ _____

❑ _____

❑ _____

❑ _____

❑ _____

❑ _____

❑ _____

❑ _____

❑ _____

Homework This Week

Write your assignments in the spaces below. Check them off as you complete them.

Reading

Mon. _____

Tues. _____

Wed. _____

Thurs. _____

Fri. _____

Language Arts

Mon. _____

Tues. _____

Wed. _____

Thurs. _____

Fri. _____

Math

Mon. _____

Tues. _____

Wed. _____

Thurs. _____

Fri. _____

Science

Mon. _____

Tues. _____

Wed. _____

Thurs. _____

Fri. _____

Social Studies

Mon. _____

Tues. _____

Wed. _____

Thurs. _____

Fri. _____

Other

Mon. _____

Tues. _____

Wed. _____

Thurs. _____

Fri. _____

Grade Record Form

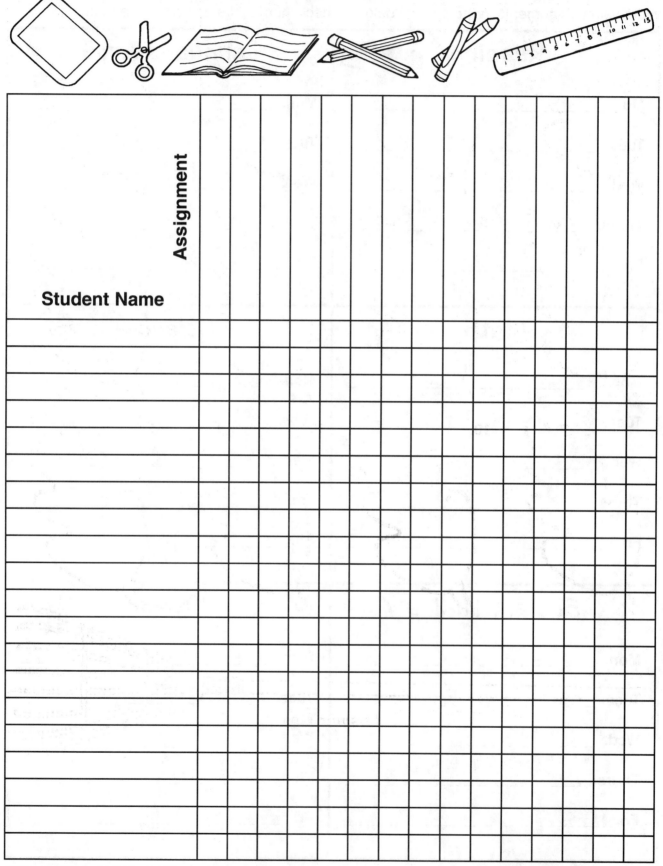

Student Name	Assignment														

Turning Over a New Leaf

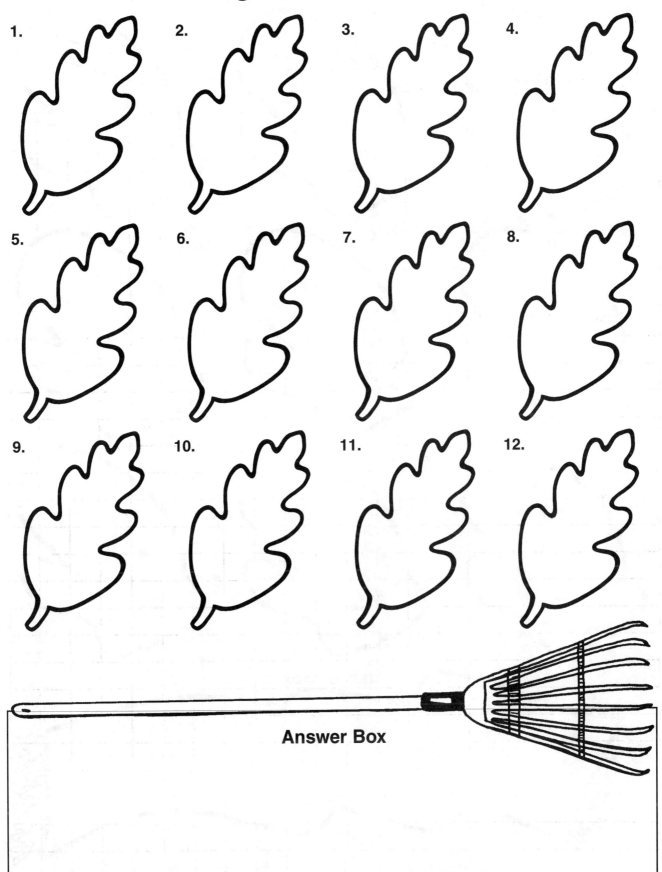

Answer Box

Fits Like a Glove

1.

2.

3.

4.

5.

6.

7.

8.

9.

Answer Box

Coming Up Roses

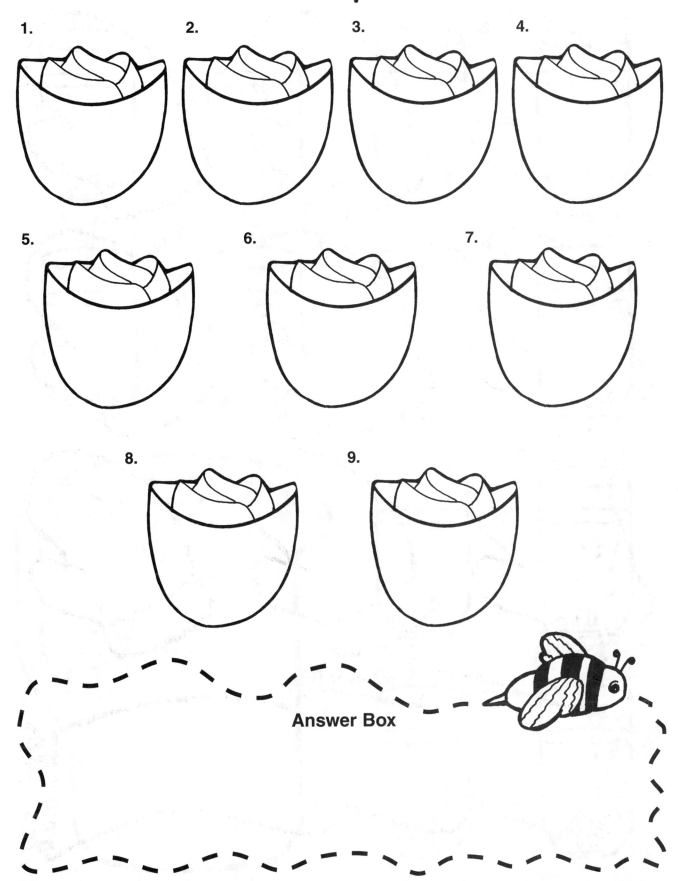

1.

2.

3.

4.

5.

6.

7.

8.

9.

Answer Box

Keeping Cool

1.
2.
3.
4.
5.
6.
7.
8.
9.
10.
11.
12.

Answer Box

Whole-Class Instruction

There are as many ways to arrange and manage a classroom as there are teachers. In this section, you will find outlined a variety of popular methods that have proven effective with many educators. Try them out to see what works for you, but by all means, adapt them as needed to suit you.

Many experts agree that teacher-directed lessons should be conducted for the whole class rather than in small groups. Dividing the class into groups decreases the teaching time to which each student is exposed. In addition, substantial amounts of seat work are necessary to keep students who are not meeting with the teacher busy and quiet (but not necessarily instructed). Whole-class instruction, however, assures that all students are exposed to the same curriculum. Students feel equal with one another because they are not separated into groups which are labeled by their abilities.

The teacher must be sure that all lessons and guided discussions have something for all students even though some parts of the lesson may be too easy or difficult for some students. The easy lesson portion gives children of all abilities a boost in self-esteem and a feeling of mastery over concepts, while portions of lessons that are difficult challenge more advanced students. Even students who do not respond at all during a lesson are usually thinking about the topic and learning from the responses of other students. Overall, whole-class instruction challenges students of all abilities and nurtures their higher-level thinking skills.

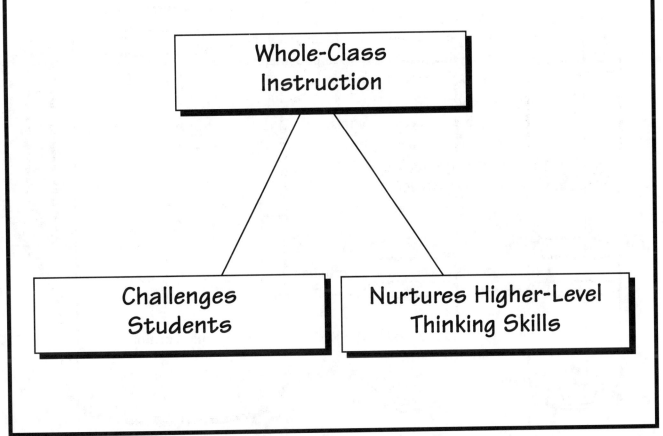

Whole-Class Instruction

Challenges Students

Nurtures Higher-Level Thinking Skills

Leading Class Discussions

Here is a list of questions and prompts that will be useful to you when leading your class in a discussion. Moreover, if you model this type of prompting, you are likely to see it reflected in the students' small group and partner discussions.

- What do you think is missing?
- What does this look like to you?
- What would we hear (smell, touch, taste, see) if we were in this situation?
- List some words and phrases that describe what you see.
- How might this look tomorrow?
- What do you think has happened?
- List as many _____ as you can think of.
- What do these have in common?
- How are these different?
- What comes after _____?
- What comes before _____?
- What would happen if _____?
- Can you think of something you would like to add?
- List these items in order from _____ to _____.
- How is this similar to that?
- What was this like before _____ happened?
- What can you identify with here?
- What would your mother (father, friend, etc.) think of this?
- What do you think is most (least) important about this?
- Who was responsible for this event?
- What caused this?
- What might happen because of this?
- Describe this in your own words.
- Who can describe this differently?
- How many ways can you _____?
- If _____ is true, then what about _____?
- How does this affect that?
- Why do you think this happened?
- How might this effect have been different?
- What could have been done to avoid this problem?
- What is missing here?
- What else do you need to know in order to understand this situation?
- How can this be improved?
- Who can think of another way?
- Where (Who, What, When) is this?

Independent Practice

Independent practice is a natural follow-up to whole-class instruction. Lessons are most effective if the materials and literature involved are made available to small groups or individuals for further investigation. Students naturally want to practice what has been presented in order to assimilate new information into their current knowledge. They want to manipulate, repeat, share, and expand upon the presented materials. Learning is a social activity. In most situations the children need classmates (no matter what the level) to bounce ideas off of and learn from. Always allow ample time and space for this valuable practice.

The teacher provides a multitude of ways to practice. This enables individual needs to be met. Centers can be set up to store the practice materials and activities. Students can then be allowed to choose or be directed to specific centers. They may work there individually or in small groups.

A few other practice exercises include journals and various other kinds of writing, sustained silent reading, rebuilding in the pocket chart, and work with individual word cards. The segment of the day labeled "open work time" is a time specifically set aside for these activities. Remember to allow students to spend several days on one activity if they wish since students learn at varying rates and extend their thoughts at different levels.

Literacy skills improve through purposeful practice. Given proper modeling, materials, and guidance, along with plenty of opportunities to practice, all students can experience literacy success.

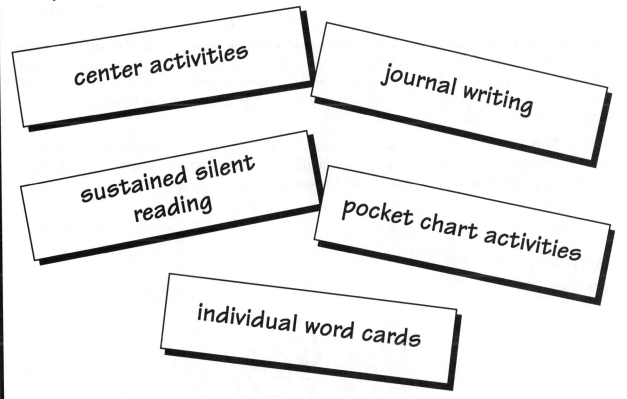

center activities

journal writing

sustained silent reading

pocket chart activities

individual word cards

Center Time

Center time can be provided every day for independent student practice. During this time, everyone is engaged in learning by interacting with an activity.

It is important to allow students to choose which activity they'd like to investigate further. Some will choose the same activity for several days if their curiosity is stimulated or if they're becoming expert at the task, which in turn builds their self-esteem. Students tend to choose activities appropriate to their ability levels because activities which are too easy or too difficult will not hold their interest. If a child is not able to choose an activity which is appropriate or productive, you may have to provide guidance.

This block of practice time is quite useful in assessing students. Teachers can hear and see what students are choosing, what they are capable of doing, what they are interested in, and how well they get along with others.

The teacher needs to provide many types of activities. He or she must also give instructions, model them, and set specific parameters for the use of each. Teachers must also be able to explain the various skills and purposes to each activity to visitors and/or parents who experience this time with the class.

Once the classroom is conducive to productive, enjoyable learning, the teacher's job is simply to monitor behavior. When students are involved and active, take the opportunity to listen and watch all of the excitement that learning brings to the classroom. If desired, keep anecdotal records of your observations.

There are many areas or activities that can be made available to the class during open work time. Remember to provide activities done previously in formal instruction. Repeating lessons and activities is a useful learning tool for students. Lower achieving students benefit from the repetition while higher achieving students will improvise and extend the learning.

The labels provided on the following pages can be duplicated and used during center time to mark each area or activity. Duplicate each twice—use one to label the area or activities and one to display as either open or closed. Using a pocket chart or double-sided masking tape, put up the labels of the areas that are open. Hang these in a place that is easily seen. The second label can be hung or placed at the area that is open for work. Children can match words or pictures to find out which areas are available. Labeling the centers open or closed gives the option of closing an activity that is being used inappropriately or needs some update or adjustment.

Finally, open work time should not be used as a reward for finishing a particular task or for good behavior. It is a fundamental part of the instructional day for each student. Students will find an activity they can perform successfully somewhere among the choices.

Center-Time Labels

Math Center

Art Center

Games and Puzzles Center

Center-Time Labels (cont.)

Drama Center

Science Center

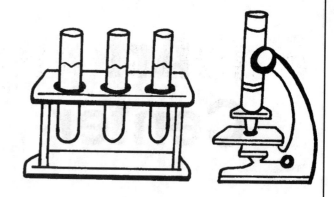

Reading Center

Cooperative Learning

Since learning language is a social activity, group interaction is an essential component of any classroom. Group activities should be a regular part of school life. Students need to learn social skills as well as academic skills. Cooperative groups can accomplish both.

Cooperative learning groups should be composed of small numbers of students of mixed abilities. In the planning for these groups, teachers should consciously include social objectives. Before beginning group work, students should understand the social, as well as the academic, objectives. As part of the assessment of the effectiveness of group work, the teacher should monitor the quality of the group interactions. A variety of instructional methods, materials, and modes of output should be encouraged so that all group members can find a way to express themselves.

A major component of the language arts is listening. This is a skill that must be developed and is imperative to learning since most instruction from teachers and classmates is oral. Group situations require members to listen actively to the speaker, understand what has been said, possibly restate what was said, and finally interpret that message in order to respond to it.

Cooperative group experiences have valuable outcomes. Children get a sense of inclusion. Students feel that they are expected to participate and that the group provides a safe environment for doing so. This makes it easier to voice opinions and take risks. The practice in reading, writing, listening, and speaking that occurs in cooperative groups is most effective among groups of students of various ability levels. In facilitating an effective classroom, the teacher must encourage and allow numerous opportunities for cooperative learning.

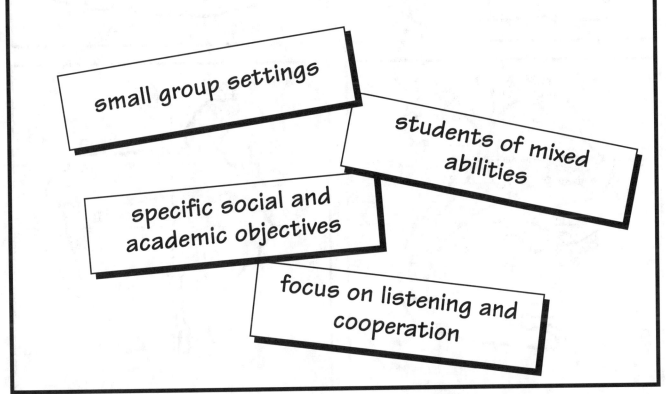

small group settings

students of mixed abilities

specific social and academic objectives

focus on listening and cooperation

Breaking into Groups

Sometimes you may want to have the students work in small groups without any particular rhyme or reason to the grouping. A fun way for students to break randomly into groups is to distribute playing cards to them. All hearts are in one group, clubs are in another, and so forth. Alternatively, the cards can be grouped by denomination so that, for example, aces through threes are in one group, fours through sixes are in another, and so on.

A similar idea is to duplicate and laminate the pictures below and then to cut apart each section. Distribute the pieces, letting the students find their "picture mates" to determine their group members for the day's activity.

Teacher Note: Duplicate this activity to help students get an idea of what it means to work together. Distribute the activity to small groups. (There are no right and wrong answers here. The idea is simply to work together to reach consensus.)

Survival

You and your group are on a small plane that suddenly crashes in a deep forest where radar cannot reach you. You survive, but the plane cannot be fixed and the radio is dead. You will have to hike through the woods, keeping in mind two things: (1) survival and (2) getting help.

Here is a list of all available supplies. Together as a group, list the supplies in order of their importance to you. Number 1 is the most important and number 20 is the least. Be prepared to explain the choices you make. Remember, you are counting on each other to survive, so everyone must agree on your decisions.

Supplies	
_____ parachute	_____ box of crackers
_____ magazine	_____ shovel
_____ rope	_____ whistle
_____ flashlight	_____ blanket
_____ softball	_____ deck of cards
_____ knife	_____ binoculars
_____ mirror	_____ rain slicker
_____ plastic bag	_____ sunscreen
_____ matches	_____ compass
_____ pencil	_____ baseball caps

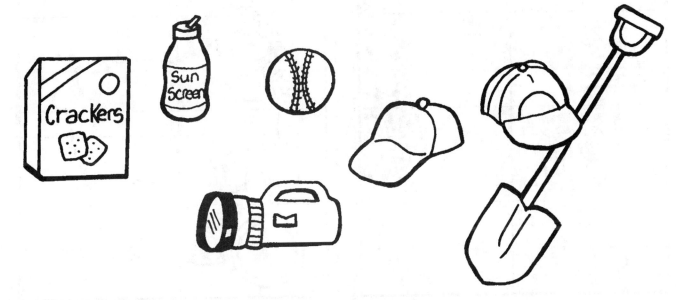

Teacher Note: *Duplicate this activity to help young students get an idea of what it means to work together. Distribute the activity to small groups. (There are no right and wrong answers here. The idea is simply to work together to reach consensus.)*

The Party

You and your group are planning a surprise party for a friend. You will need many things, but you only have enough money to buy seven. Circle the seven things below that get the most votes. Remember, everyone in your group must agree.

Party Item	Votes	Party Item	Votes

Shared Responsibility for Learning

In an effective classroom, it is clearly understood that learning is a shared responsibility among child, parents, and teacher. The following is a clear and specific outline of individual responsibilities. From it we can clearly see how all responsibilities work together for the child's best learning. Read the list yourself and if you wish, share it with parents at the start of the new school year.

The child's responsibilities are . . .

◆ to express ideas
◆ to work cooperatively with others
◆ to listen to and accept ideas of others
◆ to interact with materials, the environment, and others
◆ to ask questions and seek information and strategies to answer those questions
◆ to absorb as much language as possible through reading, writing, listening, and speaking

The parents' responsibilities are . . .

◆ to make the child responsible for daily tasks
◆ to keep the school-home relationship open and positive
◆ to spend time reading to and listening to the child every day
◆ to limit the use of electronic devices like TV and video games
◆ to be knowledgeable about the way children learn
◆ to respect the child's independence by allowing adequate time and space for his or her activities
◆ to model an enthusiasm for learning language by being readers and writers themselves
◆ to see that the child gets adequate sleep, exercise, and nutritious meals

The teacher's responsibilities are . . .

◆ to model an enthusiasm for learning and its function
◆ to create a positive and nurturing environment for students
◆ to provide a curriculum that is interesting, relevant, and purposeful
◆ to make encouraging comments which instill a "can do" attitude in students
◆ to respect students' independence by allowing adequate time and space for their interactions
◆ to provide and monitor activities integrating reading, writing, listening, and speaking, which give students valuable practice with language
◆ to keep parents informed and involved in classroom happenings
◆ to raise open-ended questions which will develop students' thinking skills and lead them to make appropriate decisions
◆ to help students express their difficulties and to suggest possible solutions

Critical Thinking

In a strong environment, children are given much control of their own learning. They are actively asking questions and seeking answers about the world. They are encouraged to use many sources of information to make guesses about solutions and to test those guesses to see if they make sense. When students are given the freedom to think about solutions to problems in a risk-free, nonjudgmental environment, they are challenged to think at higher levels. See Bloom's Taxonomy below for descriptions of the different learning levels.

Teachers must teach and model for students how to think critically rather than only teaching students the "correct answer" to a question. Use Bloom's Verbs on the next page to help you develop questions that will encourage students to think at higher levels.

Bloom's Taxonomy: Levels of Learning	
Knowledge	This level provides the child with an opportunity to recall fundamental facts and information about the story.
Comprehension	This level provides the child with an opportunity to demonstrate a basic understanding of the story.
Application	This level provides the child with an opportunity to use information from the story in a new way.
Analysis	This level provides the child with an opportunity to take parts of the story and examine these parts carefully in order to better understand the whole story.
Synthesis	This level provides the child with an opportunity to put parts from the story together in a new way to form a new idea or product.
Evaluation	This level provides the child with an opportunity to form and present an opinion backed up by sound reasoning.

Bloom's Verbs

This list of verbs below corresponds to different levels of critical thinking. Use them when creating writing assignments or asking children questions. Students' responses will help you determine the level at which they are thinking.

KNOWLEDGE		COMPREHENSION		APPLICATION	
name	recall	explain	paraphrase	transfer	apply
list	draw	summarize	review	compute	show
define	count	interpret	demonstrate	produce	change
match	identify	predict	conclude	choose	paint
label	sequence	tell	generalize	use	select
describe	quote	discuss	locate	demonstrate	prepare
recite	write	restate	identify	interview	dramatize
tell	find	illustrate	report	draw	imitate

ANALYSIS		SYNTHESIS		EVALUATION	
differentiate	compare	create	produce	judge	predict
contrast	outline	design	compose	select	rate
deduce	characterize	propose	invent	prove	choose
classify	separate	organize	pretend	decide	evaluate
debate	analyze	construct	originate	appraise	conclude
research	discriminate	develop	integrate	rank	assess
distinguish	examine	plan	rewrite	criticize	justify
relate	diagram	make up	perform	prioritize	argue

Question Mark Pattern

Use this pattern as a template. Photocopy it on brightly colored paper and cut out the question mark. Write some of Bloom's verbs on it. Use them for writing or oral discussion or select a question word (who, what, where, why, how), pose a question, and allow students to think about and express their thoughts. Students will come to see this symbol as a signal to "put their thinking caps on."

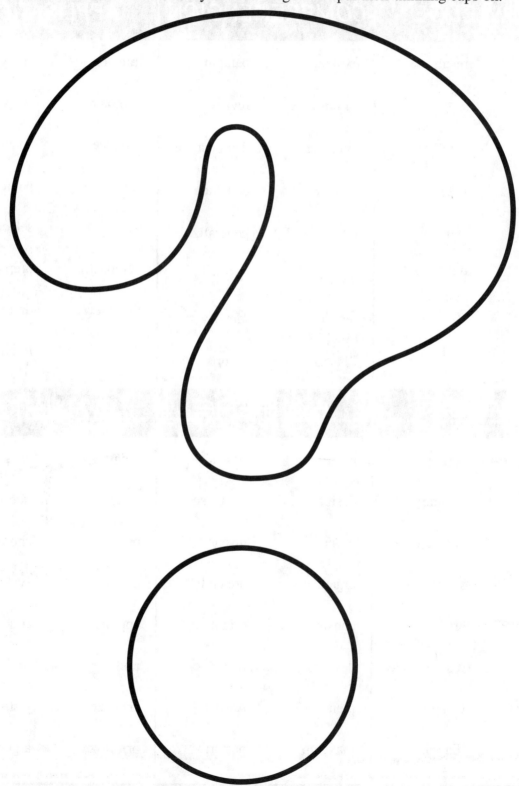

Self-Esteem Enhancement

Positive self-esteem abounds in a child-centered classroom. When curriculum is relevant and motivating, students are eager to learn. They choose independent practice at a comfortable ability level. Because they feel comfortable with their choices, students freely take risks and extend themselves. They choose to learn and feel good about their choices. Taking responsibility for learning is a foundation of a child's self-esteem.

In a healthy classroom setting, children are not individually compared. Rather, an individual's growth throughout the process of learning is recognized. Assessment is often based on observations made during actual learning situations and on a collection of work samples produced over time. Using these, a child's learning growth can be demonstrated to him/herself and others. The esteem-boosting result is, "Look how much I'm learning!"

Teachers need to ensure success for each student. If a child needs encouragement and/or prompting at a task, find a classmate who can do that. If the child constantly chooses tasks which are much too difficult, help adjust the tasks so that child will succeed. Always provide books and activities to challenge yet provide success. Too much teacher interaction will send a signal to the student that he is not capable. The child needs to feel worthy of trust and reliable. Remember that the most powerful interaction a teacher can provide a student is positive reinforcement.

Student ownership of the classroom naturally instills a positive sense of inclusion. It also creates a positive sense of obligation or commitment by each student as a member of a classroom community. This is important for class and individual self-esteem.

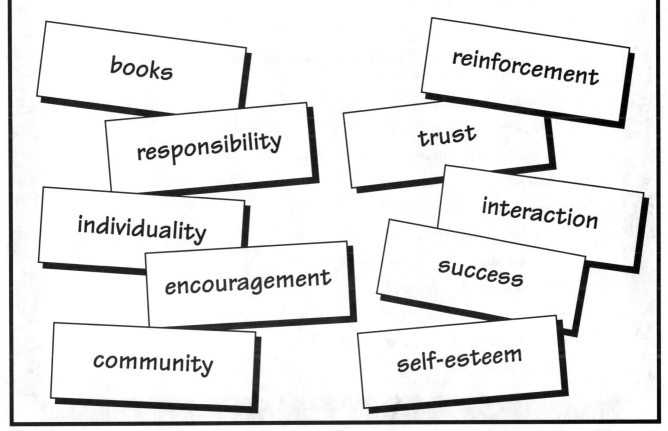

What to Say

In order to support the students' self-esteem, it is important to watch what we say and how we say it. Here are a variety of ways to say things that will show confidence in, acceptance of, and appreciation for the student and his or her work.

- I like the way you handled that.

- I'm glad you enjoy learning.

- I am glad you're pleased with this.

- Since you are not satisfied with this, do you think you can do so that you will be satisfied?

- It looks as if you enjoyed doing this.

- How do you feel about it?

- Wow! Your effort really shows here.

- You can help me by . . .

- Let's try it together.

- Knowing you, I am sure you'll do fine.

- You'll make it.

- I have confidence in you.

- That's a tough one, but I'm sure you'll work it out.

- I can understand your frustration (anger, disappointment, etc.), but I am sure you will be able to handle it.

- Thanks, you helped a lot.

- It was thoughtful of you to . . .

- Thanks, you just made my job a lot easier.

- You have a knack for . . .

- You do a good job of . . .

- I really enjoyed working with you. Thanks.

- You are always good to be around.

- You have really improved in . . .

- Yes, that's a mistake, but what can you learn from it?

- Don't give up. I know you can do it.

- Keep up this good work.

Teacher Note: Use this and the following few pages as self-esteem builders. Stress that there are no right and wrong answers.

Who Am I?

Directions: Complete the following sentences.

1. When I am grown up, I will _____.

2. A good teacher is one who _____.

3. When I need help, I can usually turn to _____.

4. Kids who break rules _____.

5. I guess I am _____.

6. I feel proud when I _____.

7. When I get in trouble, _____.

8. The nicest thing about school is _____.

9. What seems to be really unfair is _____.

10. When I feel happy, _____.

11. At home we _____.

12. My mother and I _____.

13. When I am 50 _____.

14. Kids need _____.

15. Kids should _____.

16. When I feel angry, _____.

17. My father and I _____.

18. When people criticize me, _____.

19. Most people think of me as _____.

20. When I feel sad, _____.

21. My best friend _____.

22. The people who love me don't _____.

23. Brothers and sisters _____.

24. It is no use to _____.

Values

Directions: Check the boxes under the appropriate number to show the item's importance to you. Number 1 is of the most importance to you and a 3 is the least. Number 2 is for those items that are important but not the most important to you.

Item	Importance		
	1	2	3
having many friends			
being with my family			
getting good grades			
playing well in sports			
winning a game			
having a bicycle			
being liked by my teacher			
having a best friend			
having money to spend			
staying out of trouble			
being able to make friends easily			
having many books to read			
keeping my things neat and organized			
being by myself			
spending time with a pet			
finishing my work			
being creative			
being praised by my parents			
wearing good clothes			
having a computer			

My Report Card

Directions: Grade yourself in the following areas by putting a mark in the appropriate box.

Area	Rating		
	excellent	good	poor
getting along with my classmates			
completing my classwork			
doing my best work			
following rules			
solving problems by myself			
working well with small groups			
listening to my teacher			
being neat in my work			
keeping my desk clean and organized			
doing my best printing or penmanship			
my reading ability			
my writing ability			
my math ability			
my science ability			
my art ability			
my sports ability			
completing my homework			
other (You decide.)			

Sample Floor Plans

Classroom environment is greatly affected by the arrangement of the room. Consider all your needs when arranging your room, and if the arrangement does not work for you, do not be afraid to change it. Allow yourself to be flexible, and the right plan will present itself.

Here and on the next page are two very different plans. Use them as they are or as springboards for your own ideas.

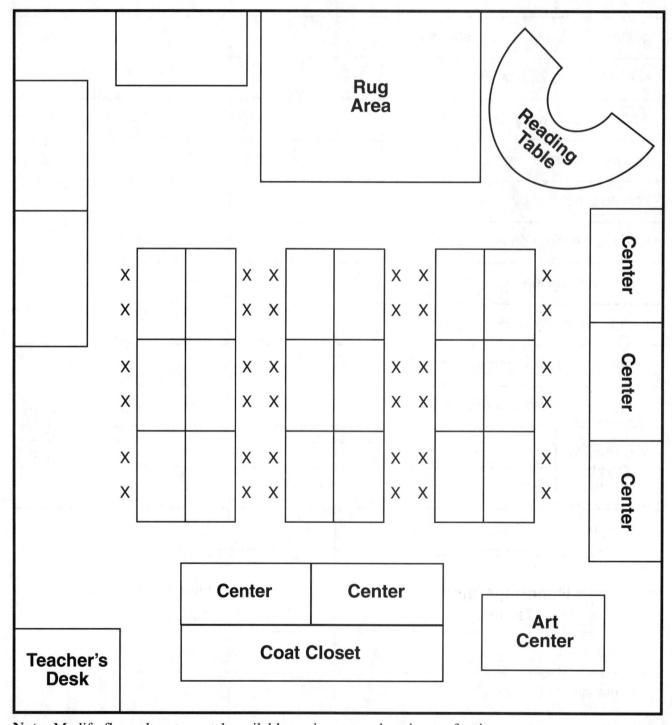

Note: Modify floor plans to match available equipment and stationary furniture.

Sample Floor Plans (cont.)

There is no rug area in this plan. It uses partner cooperative learning without moving furniture.

Front

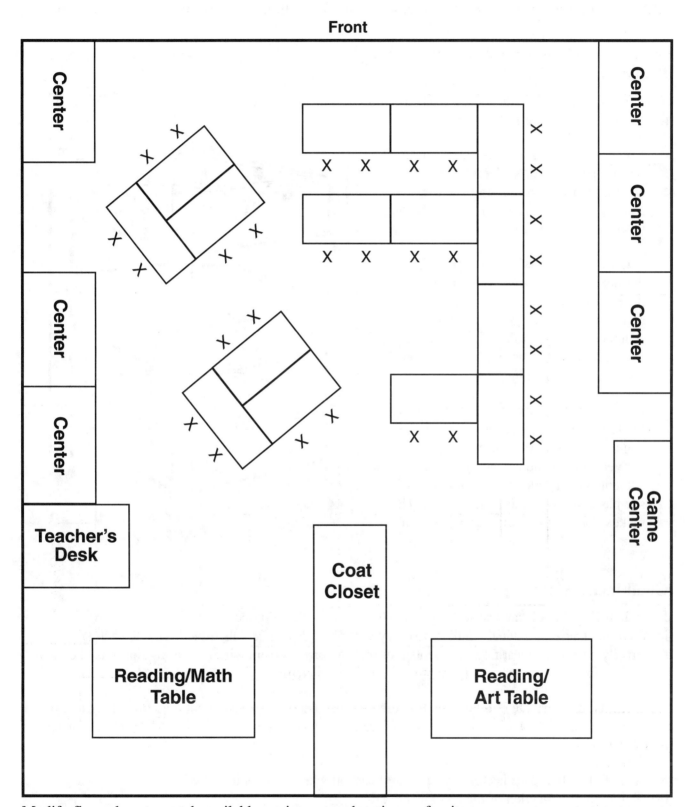

Modify floor plans to match available equipment and stationary furniture.

Getting Organized

Use the ideas on this and the following pages to organize your classroom. (**Note:** Never hesitate to ask veteran teachers how they manage their organization. You will learn many "tricks of the trade" this way.)

Paper Cart

This three-tired cart on wheels is for paper storage. It is always available to students at open work time. In it is found the following:

Lined Writing Paper—A supply of lined writing paper is for students to use in creating stories, writing notes to the teacher or to friends, reporting an incident to the suggestion box, etc.

Plain Paper—This can be regular duplicating, plain scrap, or computer paper. Children use this for the art center activities, for stamping out words and sentences with the rubber letter stamps, for stamping out coins with rubber coin stamps, or just doodling.

Extra Papers—This stack is made up for the few papers the teacher has left at the conclusion of a lesson or project. These are very useful and appealing to the student because most of the time he or she has completed this task already. This makes it a great opportunity to repeat a task for reinforcement.

Chalkboard Cart

Individual chalkboards are useful for phonics/spelling lessons, guided art, and proper handwriting instruction. These individual chalkboards (dry-erase boards can be substituted) enable each student to be actively engaged in learning. Students feel free to correct errors without fearing that mistakes will be conspicuous.

Ask parents to contribute old, large, cotton tube socks. These make excellent erasers. Chalk can be stored in the toe of the sock. These "erasers" are easily laundered by a volunteer parent about once a month.

Storage of chalkboards is best in a three-tiered cart on wheels. This mobility greatly expedites distribution and collection of the chalkboards.

Getting Organized (cont.)

"Slap" It On

To display and manipulate items like word cards, small picture cards, or name cards, tape long strips of masking tape (sticky side out) on the chalkboard or other surface. Then it's quick and easy to "slap" cards on. They can be removed, rearranged, and restuck to graph, alphabetize, categorize, etc.

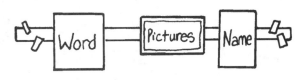

Big Book Storage

A quick and easy way to store big books is in a laundry basket. Be sure that you purchase one that is very sturdy and rectangular in shape. This ensures that your big books will stand up straight and be kept in good condition. Label the basket and keep it in the same place.

Teacher Mailbox

Obtain an old mailbox, paint it brightly, and attach it to your desk. Encourage students to write notes to you when they have something to say. The teacher mailbox is quite useful when students need to remind you of something, and it illustrates to students that writing is a necessity of life.

In-a-Bag Books

This is a great way to make quick, reusable class books. Staple together closeable, heavy-duty plastic bags on the folded ends (openings out). Use half as many bags as you have students since pages can be back-to-back. Cover the stapled edge with book tape or colored, wide plastic tape. Simply insert student-made pages. They stay clean and intact!

Getting Organized *(cont.)*

Storage Tips

Purchase flat cardboard boxes that are designed to fit under the bed for versatile storage boxes in your classroom. They are the perfect size for storage of your sentence strip stories and other pocket chart lessons. These boxes also stack nicely, making them great for storage of month-specific items like Halloween bulletin boards or art projects.

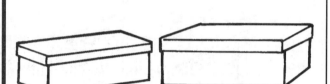

To Go Home

Designate some kind of receptacle (a drawer, a tub, or a shelf) for items to go home that day. This helps assure that nothing will be forgotten during the last few hectic minutes of the school day. Mark it clearly for substitute teachers and/or parent helpers. Give the responsibility of reminding you to check it each day to a student or a pair of students so you're doubly sure that the class has been reminded.

Interest Baskets

Use plastic baskets as book baskets. Group books of specific topics or authors together in various centers around your room. Baskets often spark interest because children know exactly where to go back for more books about a motivating topic. It also allows for the books to be displayed cover-side out, which is an exciting invitation to a child to read.

Pointer

Make a pointer available to your students during open work time. This will be used to point to and read print around the room. Be sure the pointer has a blunt or rubber tip and is used correctly. Find a convenient spot for it to be kept. This is an instant activity that the children love.

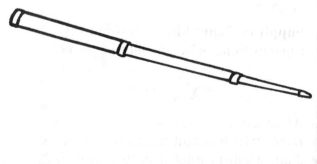

Officers and Monitors

Whether you use class officers, monitors, or a combination does not matter. The important idea is to do something to teach students responsibility for their classroom, school, and selves, including their own behavior and study habits. When the subject is first introduced, the teacher needs to teach what each monitor or officer's "job" entails so that students know what is expected. A chart with the different jobs listed on library pockets is an easy way to keep track. Write each child's name on the edge of an index note card. The cards can be put in the pockets when it is that child's turn to do a job.

It is also effective to have the students elect their own officers who in turn choose the monitors for the month, week, or other time period. This gives the students an opportunity to learn a little about an election and how to convince someone to pick them for certain jobs. Elections take time and so does teaching each officer and monitor how to do their job well. For this reason, hold elections once a month.

Here is a sample of the officers/monitors that may be used. When students have complaints, remind them that you did not pick the monitors or elect the officers and that they should try to talk with their officers about any problems. This reduces complaints and encourages the students to solve their own problems.

Officers

President—leads the class in sharing and gives table points as they get ready for recess and lunch

Vice President—takes over if the president is absent; leads the Pledge of Allegiance and takes lunch count daily

Secretary—messenger who takes notes to other classrooms and the office and helps the teacher collect homework

Monitors

Library Monitor—keeps the books in order

Line Leaders (2)—encourage students to get ready in line and walk at the front of the lines when they are ready

Art Monitors—help pass out and collect art supplies

Supply or Paper Monitors—pass out supplies from the supply tubs or teacher

Blackboard Monitor—erases the chalkboard and cleans erasers at the end of each day

Attendance Monitor—helps the teacher record who is absent and gathers books or materials that absent students may need

Pencil Monitor—sharpens extra pencils

Door Monitor—checks that the door is locked or unlocked and helps the teacher get it open and shut at the appropriate times

Light Monitor—turns the lights on when students are working in the classroom and turns them off when students leave the room

Ball or P.E. Equipment Monitor—keeps track of who gets to have the balls or other gym equipment and passes them out at the next recess or lunch

Center Monitor—checks and straightens out the centers before leaving each day

Officers and Monitors (cont.)

Cut out these icons and those on the next page and glue them to library pockets. Display them as on the diagram below. Insert index cards with the names of students who will be responsible for the jobs.

Diagram

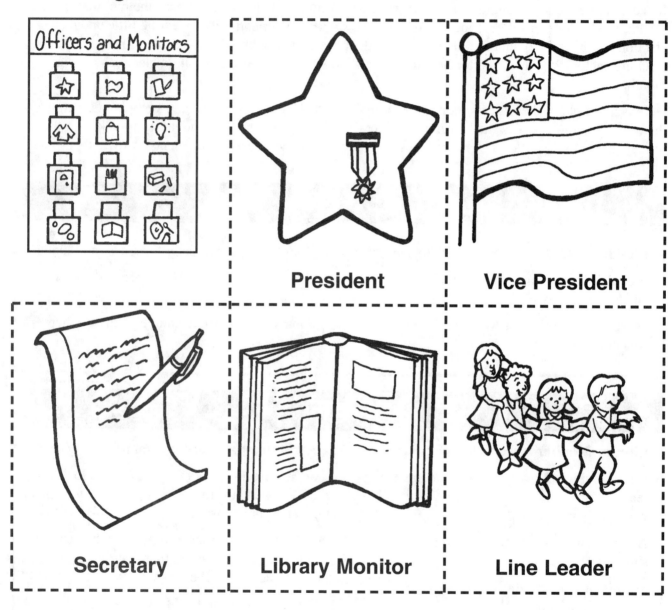

President

Vice President

Secretary

Library Monitor

Line Leader

Officers and Monitors (cont.)

Art Monitor

Supply/Paper Monitor

Board Monitor

Attendance Monitor

Pencil Monitor

Door Monitor

Light Monitor

Ball/P.E. Monitor

Center Monitor

Checking Student Work

Teachers spend a lot of time checking student work. There are several things to consider when checking student practice work. First of all, why is the work being checked? The main reasons to check practice work are to give the students feedback on how they are doing, to stop them from practicing something incorrectly, and to promote whatever is being taught. Therefore, the checking needs to be done either right after students finish the work or while they are doing the work. Spending valuable time checking a set of class papers will do little to assist learning if students do not get them back for several days. Students need immediate feedback on how they are doing. If the work is at the correct level of difficulty, students will naturally make a few errors during guided practice. This is not the time to grade for accuracy because it is practice and not mastery. You might have students check their own practice, check each other's work, or have peer tutors or parent volunteers help with checking the work so that you as the teacher can be free to teach.

The time when teachers need to check student work themselves is when students are being tested or checked for mastery of something they have been taught and after students have been given opportunities to practice and to correct errors. In other words, teachers should evaluate tests while students can often check daily work.

Returning Work
and Distributing Materials

Returning Work

There are several ways that work can be returned to students without making it a time of turmoil in the classroom. One way is to use student mailboxes. Corrected work, notes to parents, and other kinds of communications are sorted into the student mailboxes much the same as the post office does to post boxes. (Student helpers can distribute the papers.) Organizing the mailboxes in a way that makes it simple to find a particular student is the key to success here.

If you prefer, student work can be returned during sharing time. If the class meets on a rug for sharing, the students returning work can then easily put the work out on the desks. This reduces a lot of the confusion that might otherwise occur during the time when work is returned. After sharing, students simply go to their desks to put their returned papers into their notebooks or backpacks to take home.

An added bonus for having students pass out corrected work is that students have a reason to learn how to read each other's names. At the beginning of a new class, it becomes an honor to be the first to be able to read all the names in the class. The students who need help merely show the paper to someone who reads it for them.

Distributing Materials

One thing that helps the class run more smoothly is to have a plan for passing out papers, books, or other materials that are needed to complete assignments. Without a plan in mind, a lesson can really be sidetracked as the students become restless while waiting to get started between instruction and guided practice. Here are several ways to get materials to students quickly, efficiently, and with the least amount of disruption:

❏ If students sit in teams, rows, or table groups, one student can be the paper or supply monitor and be responsible for getting the materials and then distributing them to the others at his or her assigned area.

❏ Teachers can have materials ready in folders for each row, table etc. The folders can be distributed before the lesson or as they are needed. (Parent volunteers or a classroom aide can prepare the folders.)

❏ Paint pails with handles (supply tubs) are especially useful when there are materials or supplies that students need in addition to paper. Before the lesson, the teacher or student helper can put the necessary equipment inside a pail for students in a row, table, or team. Then, the teacher can locate the supply tub for easy access when needed. This method is especially helpful when using manipulative materials. For example, supply tubs will work well for a science lesson in which hand lenses, rocks, and recording sheets are needed. When it is time to use the manipulatives, it will only take seconds to distribute them.

Unexpected Interruptions

Wouldn't it be nice to be prepared for any unexpected situation? No one can be prepared for everything, but an organized teacher can have something close at hand for some of the unexpected situations that might occur at school. Some of the things you might need to be prepared for include these:

- Instructional assistants or adult volunteers are absent at the last minute so that instructional plans will have to be altered.

- Rainy days occur, and the students have to stay in at recess or lunch and will need something to do.

- Short emergencies arise where the teacher will not be able to return to the classroom for 15–30 minutes. (Have a neighboring teacher look in on the class.)

- Another teacher has an emergency, and you will need to supervise his or her class.

For situations like this, it is always a good idea to have something to fill in the time. By having a class set of a word search, coloring sheet, crossword puzzle, etc., available, someone else will be able to cover your class, or you will be able to cover another class easily.

Emergency Leave

Use the pass (provided below) when students need to leave your supervision.

Hall Pass From Room_____

Sponge Activities

A sponge activity is something that teachers give students to work on as they come into the room or to keep the students busy while the teacher takes care of necessary business like taking attendance, getting the lunch count, or collecting notes and homework. Sponge activities are also useful during transition periods when the teacher needs to help several students or to nudge someone into finishing. They are the activities or assignments that are made to "soak up" those wasted minutes when students may otherwise get out of control.

Sponge activities can be used to refocus on something students have previously learned. For example, "Use your textbooks to write down the names of the three explorers and where they explored that we talked about yesterday."

Sponge activities might also be something like a puzzle, question, or problem to solve that is used to challenge students and to keep them busy while the teacher takes care of his or her required paper work. You might challenge your class to a question a day like, "Why is the sky blue?" It gives students a chance to make suppositions about something they will (or may) study later.

Good sponge activities give students an opportunity to review, talk, or write about something they have learned. Sponges are best if they can be posted for the students to read when they are ready to complete the activity.

Draw a simple flower and label all the parts we discussed yesterday.

What Can I Do Now, Teacher?

Listed below are some suggestions for things students might do when they finish their assignments.

1. Write a story, poem, or letter.
2. Read a book.
3. Draw a picture.
4. Play a game.
5. Make a puppet.
6. Write in a journal.
7. Work a puzzle.
8. Go to a center.
9. Be a teacher's assistant.
10. Check papers.
11. Go to the school or classroom library.
12. Work on the computer.
13. Work on an extra-credit assignment.
14. Organize desk, folder, notebook and/or assignments.
15. Work on practice work sheets.
16. Use flashcards.
17. Work on another assignment with a friend.
18. Look at the class photo/activity album.
19. Read one of the class-written collections or big books.
20. Read the walls of the classroom.
21. Read journal.
22. Make a cartoon story.
23. Write a commercial.
24. Write a weather report.
25. Write a sports story.
26. Draw a map.
27. Use manipulatives to demonstrate or practice math problems.
28. Play with clay.
29. Listen to a favorite story or song.
30. Make an art project.
31. Work on a science experiment.
32. Read magazines.
33. Make a game board.
34. Make a banner.
35. Make flashcards.
36. Work on a class newspaper.

Name

finished all assignments today! Three cheers!!!

Teacher's Name   Date

Library Pass

Name:

Date:

Return by:

Teacher's Name:

Twenty Super Sponge Activities

1. Play 5 x 5. This is easily accomplished by making a grid of 25 squares. Choose five categories. Place one on the top of each box. Then randomly choose five letters and place one on each box down the side. Have students call out words that fit each category. This is really handy when working with a theme that you wish to review.

2. Charades are a fun sponge, especially as a review. Use spelling or vocabulary words, titles of books by authors the class has studied, or activities going on in school. Put these on slips of paper and place in a container. Let individuals or groups of students choose one and act it out.

3. Read aloud to your class! Keep some funny, short stories or a book of limericks available for a quick read.

4. Play "baseball." Choose a skill that needs to be reviewed. Draw a baseball diamond on the board. Choose a scorekeeper. Divide the class into two teams. Determine which team is up first. Ask each player a review question. If the player answers correctly, have him or her run the bases by marking the base on the diamond on the board. A run is scored every time a player touches home base. If the team misses three questions, the other team is up.

5. Try some rhythms. Clap or tap out a rhythm and then have students repeat it. Vary the patterns and the lengths, making them increasingly more challenging.

6. Choose a category such as food, movies, or places, and challenge students to think of one for each letter of the alphabet.

7. Select a category such as famous people. Have one student say the name. The next student must name another famous person whose first name begins with the last letter of the person's name (for example, George Bush, Harriet Tubman, Nancy Reagan).

8. Ask students a number of questions such as: Is there anyone whose phone number digits add up to 30? or Whose birthday is closest to the date when man first walked on the moon (or any other date you have been studying)? or If you add the ages of everyone in your family, who has the highest number? Who has the lowest?

9. Create a spelling chain. All students stand. Give them a spelling word. The first person says the first letter, the second gives the second letter, and so on. If a student gives the wrong letter, he/she must sit down.

10. Play "guess the characteristic." Ask several students who all have something in common to stand. The class, including the standing students, must guess what they all have in common, such as they all have shoes with no laces, they all walk to school, or they are all in band.

11. Do a daily edit to start the day or fill small spaces of time. These become writing skill mini-lessons. Lift an incorrect sentence directly from students' writing or create one including errors that students are commonly making. You may wish to focus on one skill at a time. Print the incorrect sentence(s) on the board or overhead. Have students edit the sentence and write it correctly in a section of their journals or a special notebook that can be used for reference. Follow up at some time during the day with a class discussion so the students can finalize their corrections and see that there may be more than one way to solve a writing problem.

Twenty Super Sponge Activities *(cont.)*

12. An especially effective daily edit that promotes more interesting writing is Expand a Sentence. Give students a very simple sentence (e.g., The child ran.) Include insert marks where you want students to add words and underline words that they may change to something more exciting. Model an expansion for students the first time you do this activity. The new sentence may become: The very excited young lady raced wildly down the street with her red braids flying straight out behind.

13. Keep a supply of board and table games that require strategy and thinking. Use them for special fill-in times like rainy day recesses. Good examples are Scrabble, Monopoly, Boggle, and Chutes and Ladders.

14. Collect word searches, crossword puzzles, kids' pages from Sunday comics, and Mad Libs. Laminate them for wipe-off reuse.

15. Save about-to-be discarded paper with at least one blank side (computer printouts, old dittos, faded construction paper, etc.) Use for free-drawing time. Also encourage students to free-write; many of them also improve creativity and expertise in drawing with practice.

16. Derive many words from one. Copy on the blackboard a multi-syllabic word taken from a theme or topic of the day. Ask students to write as many words from this as they can in a specified time. Only letters from the original word may be used. This activity can be done in small groups or individually.

17. Set up a magnetic board center for sponge activities. Divide the board into "yes" and "no" columns. Prepare a magnetic name tag for each student by gluing a tagboard square with the student's name onto a piece of magnetic strip (available at fabric or sign stores). On the board pose daily questions which involve critical thinking, opinions, or problem-solving activities. The questions must have either a yes or no answer. Have students place their magnetic name tags in the appropriate column. Discuss responses.

18. Read a short story, poem, essay, news articles, etc., to the class. Have students write a short first impression of it. Compare student responses.

19. Play "Three-in-a-Row." Make game boards from 8 ½" x 11" pieces of tagboard, cardboard, or index paper. Divide each game board into nine equal boxes. Provide X and O cards (five of each) for each game board. (Be sure the cards fit into the boxes.)

    Two students use one game board; one using X cards and the other using O cards. Use this game for reinforcement or review. When a student responds correctly to a problem or activity, he/she places a card in a box. If incorrect, the player loses a turn. The first player to achieve three in a row vertically, horizontally, or diagonally is the winner.

20. Incorporate a "Brainteaser Time" into your day. Choose from a selection of brainteaser activities or have students make up some of their own. These can be presented to the class as part of your daily sponge activities.

Calendar Puzzle

Directions: Find the seven days of the week and the 12 months of the year in this puzzle. Circle them. You will need to know the days and months for use in your homework calendar.

```
H T F P S Y A D S R U H T K H D S R T K
S K G F U R T A K R J K P Y R D S W R M
A H O T E W P B X C D M I Y C X Z D R A
T G F G N R C X R D X M V L F E W E H R
U D R L I L L K G V R R T U R D E B R C
R M H L S W M O N D A Y W J V B D E E H
D A J F I K H L B U F G H C K D N R B E
A D J A N U A R Y F H J J D F W E N M J
Y R E F G J K R R E B M E T P E S E E E
R E H Y A M K L U T R R D H J D D N C M
C B K K J G F U Y H K L S V X Z A M E R
A M N R E T U E S D A Y Y U G J Y V D S
Z E M E R B J F L D E C A U G U S T A H
X V H J F J F Y E N N H D Y G C T U T H
J O D F F O C T O B E R B F G T S R M Y
K N N B V R V C N T R G D H K J A I Y A
W H D S Y O I P O W E U B M E R J S T D
S A T G H D I D R T W D A D B P X E P N
D I A L J G U O A P E O N R T R E S P U
J U N E A V C X Z Y T I E A Y O K I L S
```

Days		Months		
Monday	Friday	January	May	September
Tuesday	Saturday	February	June	October
Wednesday	Sunday	March	July	November
Thursday		April	August	December

Message-Go-Round

Directions: Starting with the circled letter "D" at the upper left hand corner, write every other letter written around the picture on the lines below. The result will be a famous proverb.

Ⓓ T O R N D T K P O U Y T U O W F D F

Draw a picture of something you need to do.

D <u>O</u> __ __ __ __ __ __ __ __ __ __ __ __ __ __

__ __ __ __ __ __ __ __ __ __ __ __ __ __ __

__ __ __ __ __ __ __ __ __ __ __ __ __ __.

Discipline Strategies

Discipline with Dignity

All students need to be treated with dignity. Even when a student is being disciplined, he or she needs to retain dignity. Private reminders and conferences with the child will preserve his or her dignity and yours.

One of the best things to remember concerning disciplining students is that they win whenever they get you to "lose your cool." Take your time when students "push your buttons" and decide carefully on your response. In this way, you will not behave in a way that you will regret later.

Teach Students Responsibility

Students need to be taught that they are responsible for their own behavior. If a student does not follow the rules it is best for natural or determined consequences to take their course whenever possible. When parents and others intervene, they take the responsibility for the student's behavior away from the student.

Exercise Break

One of the best favors you can do for your students and yourself when students get wiggly and cannot seem to concentrate is to take an exercise break. One good time for a break like this is about 45 minutes before lunch. Take your students outside for 5–7 minutes of exercise led first by yourself, and then, after they know the exercises, the students. This is not to replace physical education, but it is a quick chance to do some specific physical activity when students need it most.

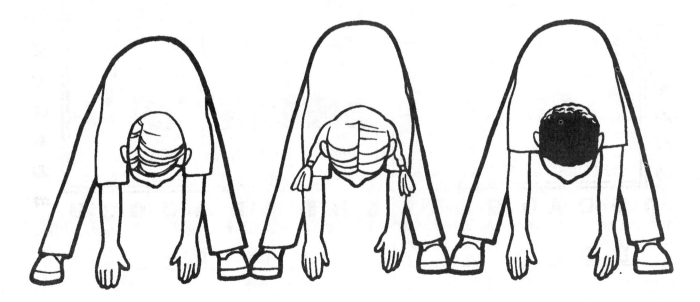

Another variation on this is to use low impact aerobics for children in the classroom. (For example, Walt Disney produces a record called *Mousercise* which is excellent.) One caution is that many of the shoes the students wear to school might be dangerous for exercise routines. If this is the case, you might want to encourage students to bring some tennis shoes to school for their exercise breaks.

Color System

Here is a very simple system for classroom behavior management. A letter explaining this system is provided on page 102. The color system involves the use of a color chart. Simply provide a pocket chart with a pocket for each student. Label the pockets with the students' names. Prepare cards for the pockets in the following colors:

green—excellent citizenship

yellow—warning for improper behavior

orange—transgression meriting loss of one recess or a time-out to think about actions

purple—transgression(s) with more serious consequences (such as loss of day's recesses, clean-up detail, loss of a privilege, etc.)

red—transgression requiring parental contact to remedy situation

Provide a color card for each student each day. Keep a record chart showing each student's color at the end of the day. At the end of the week, any student showing only yellows can be rewarded with a small prize or treat. If the entire class has only greens for 10 consecutive days (or another number determined by you), you might consider celebrating the behavior with a simple class party or video.

With this system you can reinforce positive behavior while allowing the students to monitor themselves. (They will learn immediately what the colors mean!) If any student persists in negative behavior, contact his or her parents immediately. There is no reason for delay. Remember, you, the parents, and the child are partners in education.

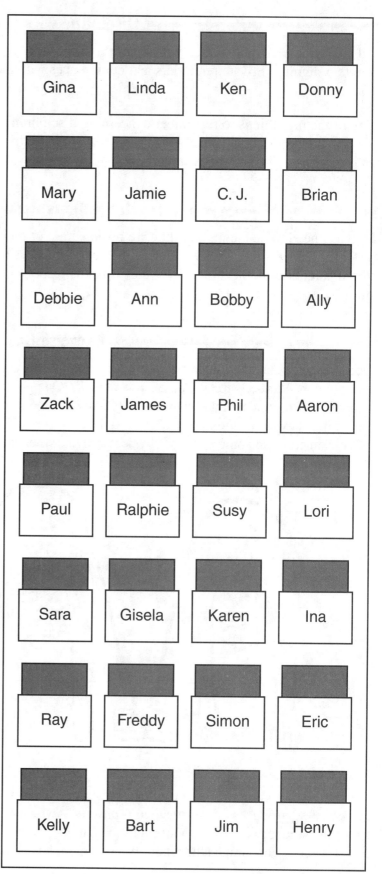

Attention or Quiet Signals

What do you use to get the attention of your students when they are working? It's hard for the "teacher look" to work when they are happily working on a group activity or not looking at you and talking as they work. One of the best treats a teacher can do for herself is to teach her class one or two signals for when she wants the attention of her students. You need several signals because if the class is quiet, one signal might work, but if they are noisy or on the playground, you may need a different signal altogether. The other key is that you need to teach the signal just as you would a math problem or a vocabulary word. After you have taught the signal, the students will need time and opportunity to practice it. If their practice is great, tell them so. If it is not, tell them they will need to practice the signal again until they can do it just right and mean it. If you accept less than complete attention, that is just what they will learn to give you. You may need to practice occasionally if they slip.

When deciding on the signal for your class, consider the age, grade, ability level, and maturity of the group. Just because it worked with the same grade level last year does not mean it will work well with this group.

Listed below are some possible signals.

Raised Hand	**Turning off the Lights**
Teacher raises her hand, and then the students stop talking, look at the teacher, and raise their hands until the class is ready.	Students stop working and talking and put their heads down. 
Bell, Piano Chord, or Musical Tone	**Clapped Rhythm**
Students stop and look at the teacher until everyone is ready. 	Teacher claps a rhythm, and the students clap either a responding rhythm or repeat what the teacher clapped and then look at the teacher.

Whistle Signal

Students freeze and look at the teacher.

Reaching Behavior and Discipline Goals

Most behavior and discipline programs with elementary children include some kind of positive reinforcement reward that the students are working toward. In order to make the reward something that seems special, you might want to let parents know that students have reached their goal and what the reward is.

Many teachers use popcorn as a treat and combine it with a chance for students to read books or play games of their choice. This does not cost much, and yet students enjoy it. Students will often choose one of several school-type activities as long as they can eat a cup of popcorn while doing it. If you do not wish to pop the corn, buy a large bag of pre-popped popcorn and a package of inexpensive paper cups to use as scoops and dishes. Students can volunteer to bring large cans of fruit juice or just drink water.

Sample Certificate for Reaching Behavior and Discipline Goals

Time To Celebrate

We have reached our goal and will be having a
popcorn party on_____! Students may
bring games to play that are appropriate for school.
Please see that the student's name is on the game
and that it is brought to school in a paper or plastic
bag.

Thanks for your help!

Awards and Rewards

Rewards that you can use at school fall into three major categories—recognition, privileges, and tangible rewards. No single kind of reward works better than another. Select rewards for students based on the grade level and preferences of the students. This is but a partial list of the kinds of rewards you might decide to use. Be sure to add your own ideas as you think of them.

Privileges

- lunch with the teacher
- library pass
- computer time
- pass for skipping homework
- tutor other students
- special art project
- special helper for the day
- choice of some activity
- work on a special project, game, center, etc.

Recognition

- telephone call to parents
- name in class or school newspaper
- hug, smile, or pat on the back
- display work
- class cheer, chant, etc.
- student of the day, week, month
- note sent home to parents
- announcement to the class
- recognition in daily announcements or at flag ceremony

Tangible Rewards

- stars
- popcorn party
- stickers
- paper bookmarks
- bonus points or extra credit
- educational video or movie
- snacks/treats in the classroom
- grab bag or treasure chest
- stamp for ink pad
- pencil, eraser, pencil top
- tokens for no homework, extra recess, etc.

Discipline Checklist

❏ Have your lessons clearly planned so students do not experience "down time."

❏ Keep parents informed about your class activities, discipline plan, homework, and how they can support your program.

❏ Set up simple, clear class rules and teach them to the students.

❏ Have both consequences and rewards for appropriate/inappropriate behavior established with students.

❏ Communicate with parents early when a student is having problems at school.

❏ Follow school policy concerning suspensions, keeping students after school, and limiting recess or lunch time.

❏ Be consistent, fair, and positive with students.

❏ Plan how to reward students for completing work assignments.

❏ Help students to feel successful, and they won't need to use disruptions or negative behavior for attention.

❏ Plan what students are to do if they have trouble completing their work or if they finish early.

❏ Consider alternating between quiet, individual activities and more energetic group activities.

Behavior and Work Contracts

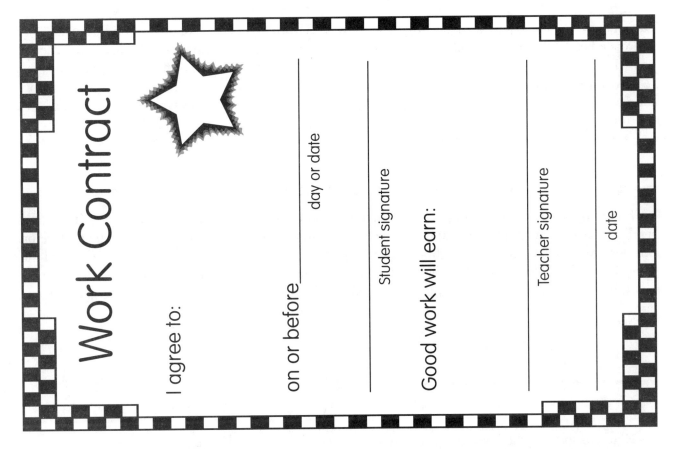

Work Contract

I agree to:

_____
on or before _____ day or date

_____
Student signature

Good work will earn:

_____
Teacher signature

_____
date

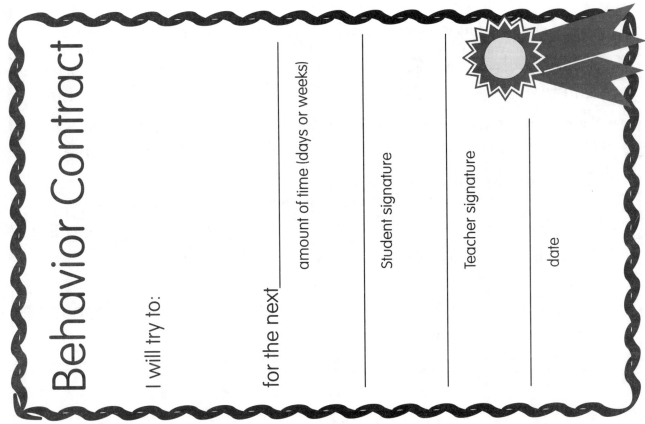

Behavior Contract

I will try to:

_____
for the next _____ amount of time (days or weeks)

_____
Student signature

_____
Teacher signature

_____
date

The Substitute

Teachers get sick, have an unexpected delay, or have other problems just like other workers. The difference between most jobs and teaching is that there are about 30 children depending on the teacher even when he or she is not there. Many other jobs can wait until the return of the worker, but this is not the case with teaching. Discussed in this section will be the Emergency Substitute Folder and a set of materials to help the substitute "get by" for a day if you are unexpectedly away. The other type of substitute materials discussed here will be substitute plans for when you know ahead of time you will not be with your students (for teacher training, in-service, etc.).

Emergency Substitute Folder

The following pages should be duplicated, filled out, and updated each year for your class. They can then be glued to a manila folder and either given to the school secretary or left in a prominent place on your desk in the event that they might be needed. In addition to what is written on the pages glued on the folder, certain things should be included inside the folder that will make a substitute's life run more smoothly. Usually when the substitute has a good day, so does your class, and they are easier to get started with again when you return.

Here are some of the items to include in an emergency substitute folder.

- **generic math assignment**—either computation or problem solving—that most, if not all, of the students can use for practice (This should be a practice sheet that students will enjoy completing. Choose something that the students think is fun because it looks like a puzzle or a game.)

- **literature selection**—to be read orally to the class (Write down a few extension ideas for writing and a related art assignment.)

- **physical education games**—ones that the class knows (It is usually best if you don't suggest something the substitute won't know the rules for unless a set of rules is also included.)

- **special directions** for rainy, assembly, or minimum days

- **map of the school**

- **current class list and seating arrangement**

The Substitute *(cont.)*

Regular Substitute Plans

When you know ahead of time that you will have to be away from your class, you need to leave plans that are more detailed than you probably write for yourself. Some of the notes and page numbers that might be enough for you will need to be clarified for a substitute. Preparing a step-by-step plan for the day may take extra time, but it will be worth it if you do not have to reteach what should have been taught while you were away.

Leave the Emergency Substitute Folder whenever you are going to be absent, but caution the substitute to use your regular plans if at all possible. There is a lot of information in the substitute folder that will be helpful in either case.

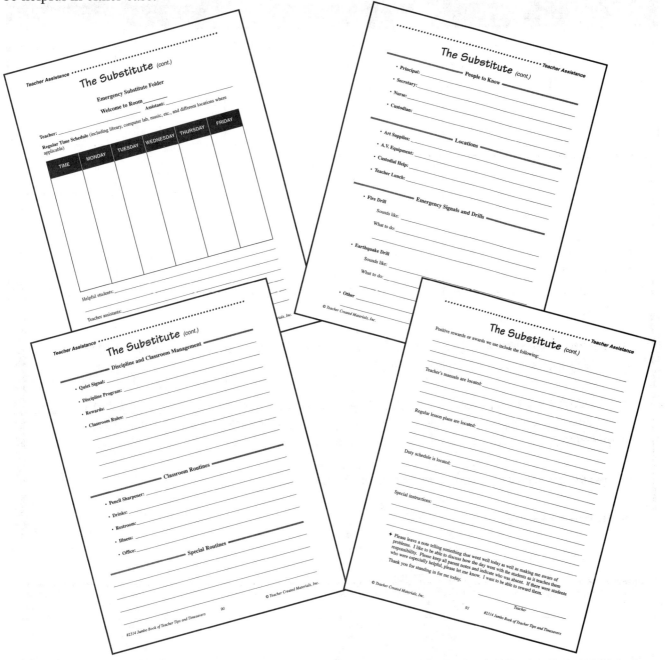

The Substitute *(cont.)*

Emergency Substitute Folder

Welcome to Room_____

Teacher: _____   **Assistant:** _____

Regular Time Schedule (including library, computer lab, music, etc., and different locations where applicable)

TIME	MONDAY	TUESDAY	WEDNESDAY	THURSDAY	FRIDAY

Helpful students: _____

_____

Teacher assistants: _____

_____

Children with special needs or health problems: _____

_____

The Substitute *(cont.)*

People to Know

- **Principal:** _____

- **Secretary:** _____

- **Nurse:** _____

- **Custodian:** _____

Locations

- **Art Supplies:** _____

- **A.V. Equipment:** _____

- **Custodial Help:** _____

- **Teacher Lunch:** _____

Emergency Signals and Drills

- **Fire Drill**

    Sounds like: _____

    What to do: _____

    _____

- **Earthquake Drill**

    Sounds like: _____

    What to do: _____

    _____

- **Other** _____

    _____

The Substitute *(cont.)*

Discipline and Classroom Management

- **Quiet Signal:** _____

- **Discipline Program:** _____

- **Rewards:** _____

- **Classroom Rules:** _____

  _____

  _____

  _____

  _____

Classroom Routines

- **Pencil Sharpener:** _____

- **Drinks:** _____

- **Restroom:** _____

- **Illness:** _____

- **Office:** _____

Special Routines

_____

_____

_____

_____

The Substitute *(cont.)*

Positive rewards or awards we use include the following: _____

_____

_____

_____

Teacher's manuals are located: _____

_____

_____

_____

Regular lesson plans are located: _____

_____

_____

_____

Duty schedule is located: _____

_____

_____

_____

Special instructions: _____

_____

_____

_____

✦ Please leave a note telling something that went well today as well as making me aware of problems. I like to be able to discuss how the day went with the students as it teaches them responsibility. Please keep all parent notes and indicate who was absent. If there were students who were especially helpful, please let me know. I want to be able to reward them.

Thank you for standing in for me today.

_____
Teacher

Parent Volunteers

Thank goodness for parent volunteers! They can be of help in so many ways. If you take the time to get organized, you will find your work load tremendously eased if you make use of the wonderful and generous support of your classroom parents.

Communicators

Forms to use to keep the activities of your volunteers organized can be found on the following two pages. In the Communicators section of the book, you will find a variety of notes to send home to recruit volunteers and parental assistance. Do not be afraid to use these! It never hurts to ask.

What to Do

Parents can help in many ways if you let them. Here are some ideas.

- Monitor learning centers.
- Provide one-on-one assistance with a struggling student.
- Take down and put up bulletin boards.
- Check and correct objective papers.
- Duplicate work sheets and communicators, and forms.
- Return student work.
- Collect student work.

- Restock supplies.
- Trace and cut patterns.
- Attach clip art to letters and forms.
- Type or input student writing for publishing.
- Read aloud stories.
- Teach a lesson for which they are experts. (**Note:** You must always supervise. Never leave a parent in charge of your class!)

Room Parents

Room moms and dads are traditionally the party planners and organizers. Work with them to arrange party activities, games, and treats. You decide on how much responsibility you wish to turn over. For example, you can let them arrange everything, you can provide guidelines, or you can ask them to carry out the plans you arrange. It is always the teacher's decision. The benefits of allowing parents to organize the parties are that they get a sense of shared responsibility for the activity of the classroom and a great deal of extra responsibility is lifted from your shoulders.

Classroom parties traditionally fall on holidays such as Halloween, Valentine's Day, St. Patrick's Day, and so forth. Also, there are usually parties on the day before a vacation such as winter break and, of course, the last day of school. If your school does not have a policy for party days (and most do), you decide on the frequency and times.

It is also a nice idea to plan parties for the end of an extended unit of study. These parties should be academically based. Students can share their work with other faculty, classes, or their parents. Simple refreshments can be served. It is especially nice if the refreshments reflect the unit of study. For example, nuts and berries after studying a unit on bears would be apropos and fun for the students.

Sign-In Sheet

Welcome! Thank you for helping in our classroom. Please sign your name and date each time you work in the room. Also, record how many hours you worked. Thank you for your hard work. It is appreciated by all of us.

Name	Date	Hours

Volunteer Activities

Use this form to keep track of the work you do in the classroom. Please work on anything marked with an asterisk (*) first. Write down any comments, concerns, or problems you have had with these projects. Thank you!

Project	Started	Completed
Project:		
Comments:		
Project:		
Comments:		
Project:		
Comments:		
Project:		
Comments:		
Project:		
Comments:		
Project:		
Comments:		

When Your Day Is Done

Here are a variety of survival tips to keep even the busiest teacher fresh and focused.

Clocking Out

One of the best things about teachers is that the profession becomes part of who they are. Students, curriculum, upcoming events—these are with them night and day. That can also be a problem. Like everyone else, teachers need balance. Learn to do the work of the day, finish it, and go home to another part of life. If possible, set a time to leave the school each afternoon and try to complete all necessary paperwork and plans before you leave. Ideally, plans for a coming week are prepared well in advance, but at the very least the plans are set by quitting time on Friday. Organization will help, but the key is keeping a healthy attitude about balance. When it is time to leave, do so, and put the work behind you.

Journals

It is a good idea to jot down some highlights and questions about your day after the children leave. This will help you in a variety of ways, including keeping your thoughts clear and bringing to light some possible solutions to persistent difficulties. Your journals can also be useful when conferencing with students and parents. The writing will help you to be prepared and clear, providing details and examples of the points you are trying to make.

Peer Time

Spend time every day meeting and talking with fellow teachers, if only briefly and casually. It is easy to become isolated in a classroom. Talking with others and sharing experiences and concerns will help to keep you positive and motivated.

Communicating with Parents and Students

There are many times throughout the year when you will need or want to send written communications to parents and students. However, sometimes it is difficult to find the exact words you want when you need them. Other times, you simply do not have the time to compose the right communication.

On the following pages you will find a vast array of form letters and written incentives. By duplicating them and filling in any missing information, you can use the communicators as is. However, you may wish to type them on your own stationery or to write them in your own longhand, particularly if they are sensitive in nature. Sending a letter of condolence with blanks filled in will certainly take away from the feelings of respect and concern that you wish to communicate.

Getting Ready

Before the school year starts, it may be wise (and ultimately timesaving) to enter each of the letters into your own word-processing program. In this way, you will have them ready when you need them, and you will be able to edit them immediately to suit each need as it arises. The letters are yours to use in any way you choose so feel free to adapt them as you wish.

One More Tip

With the previous tip comes another. Anything you can do during the summer or other break times to get ready for the school year will prove enormously beneficial in the long run. Time spent up front will save countless time in the future, and moreover, the time it saves will be time you cannot spare once the school year is under way. This will prove true for your communications as well as for countless other areas.

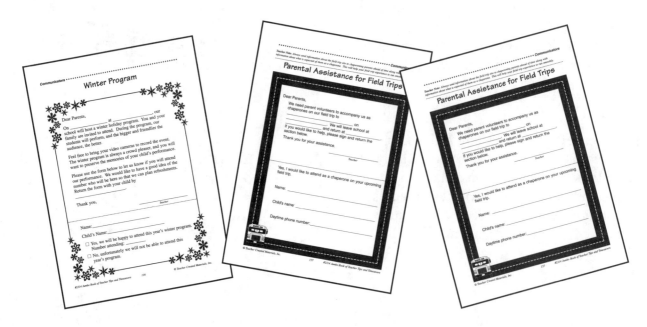

Introductory Letter to Parents

Dear Parents,

I am pleased to take this opportunity to introduce myself to you and to welcome your child to my class. A good learning experience is built on a cooperative effort among parent, child, and teacher. I look forward to the work and growth we will all accomplish this year.

My expectations for conduct and academic standards are high. With your participation both in and out of the classroom, we can look forward to a productive, creative, and enjoyable year together. In the past, I have had many parents volunteer their time in the classroom, and I encourage this because it provides opportunities for more children to receive personal attention. If you are interested in volunteering, please let me know. This can be done on a weekly, bi-weekly, or occasional basis. Any help you can give will be warmly appreciated.

You can also help by providing me with any information that will aid me in better understanding your child. Some things I am interested in include the following:

- Important experiences that may be affecting your child's state of mind (death in the family, a best friend moving away, loss of a pet, etc.)
- Special medical needs
- Study habits at home
- Television viewing habits
- After-school activities and special interests
- Feelings toward school
- Conflicts among family members

Although I am interested in anything that could be affecting your child, it is not necessary for you to reveal personal information. Please know that anything you do say will be kept in the strictest confidence.

Again, welcome! Please feel free to contact me about any questions or concerns you may have. My classroom door is always open, and messages can be left for me with our school secretary, to which I will respond as soon as possible.

Sincerely,

_____

Request for Information

Dear Parents,

To help me know more about your child, I would appreciate your help in completing the sentences below and a short descriptive paragraph about your child on the back of this paper. Please, return this form to me by _____.

Thank you for assisting me in getting acquainted with your child.

Sincerely,

_____

Child's Name: _____

Parents' Names: _____

Date: _____

My child likes to be called _____.

My child likes to _____

_____

_____.

The thing my child enjoys about school is _____

_____

_____

My child participates after school in _____

_____

_____.

One thing I really enjoy about my child is _____

_____.

Philosophy of Education

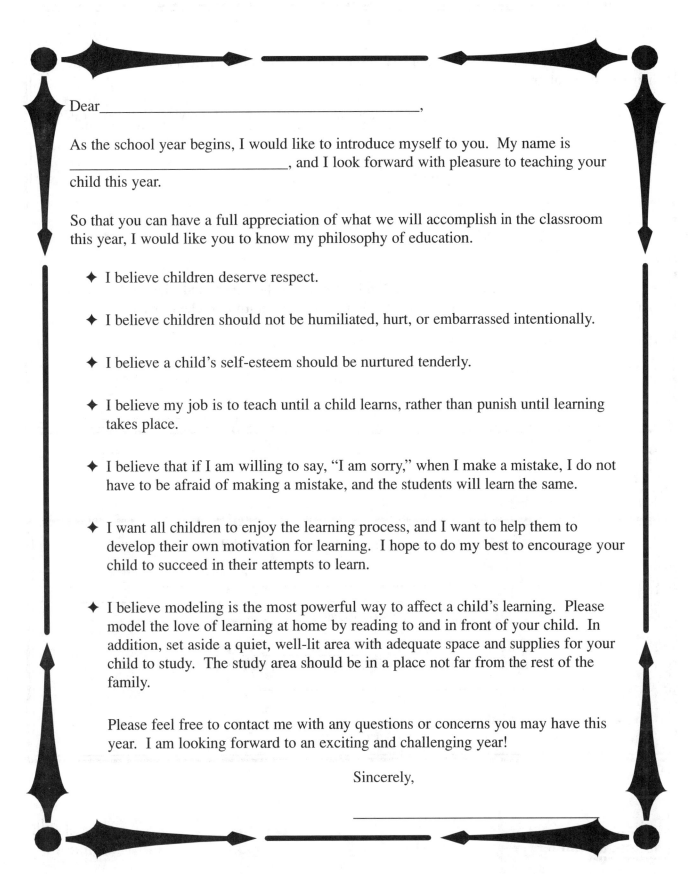

Dear_____,

As the school year begins, I would like to introduce myself to you. My name is
_____, and I look forward with pleasure to teaching your
child this year.

So that you can have a full appreciation of what we will accomplish in the classroom
this year, I would like you to know my philosophy of education.

✦ I believe children deserve respect.

✦ I believe children should not be humiliated, hurt, or embarrassed intentionally.

✦ I believe a child's self-esteem should be nurtured tenderly.

✦ I believe my job is to teach until a child learns, rather than punish until learning
takes place.

✦ I believe that if I am willing to say, "I am sorry," when I make a mistake, I do not
have to be afraid of making a mistake, and the students will learn the same.

✦ I want all children to enjoy the learning process, and I want to help them to
develop their own motivation for learning. I hope to do my best to encourage your
child to succeed in their attempts to learn.

✦ I believe modeling is the most powerful way to affect a child's learning. Please
model the love of learning at home by reading to and in front of your child. In
addition, set aside a quiet, well-lit area with adequate space and supplies for your
child to study. The study area should be in a place not far from the rest of the
family.

Please feel free to contact me with any questions or concerns you may have this
year. I am looking forward to an exciting and challenging year!

Sincerely,

_____

Classroom Rules

Dear Parents,

We are off to a good start for the school year. The children are enthusiastic and eager to tackle their new curriculum.

To help ensure a successful school experience, we have developed the following classroom rules:

Please review our class rules with your child to be sure he or she understands them fully. Both you and your child should sign the tear-off section below and return it to class tomorrow.

Thank you for your support.

Sincerely,

_____

I have reviewed the class rules with my child.

_____
Parent signature

I understand the rules and will try to follow them this school year.

_____
Student signature

School Discipline Plan

_____
School name

School Discipline Plan

Prohibited Behavior

Parental support is needed and appreciated to encourage children to observe school rules and

procedures. _____is glad to work closely with parents to teach and

maintain responsible student behavior. Through communications with your child's teacher, you will

remain well informed and actively involved in your child's education. Please review this plan with your

child and then sign below. Thank you for your support and cooperation.

Sincerely,

_____

- -

We have read and will support_____School's Discipline Plan.

School name

Room_____   Date_____

_____   _____
Student Signature   *Parent Signature*

Classroom Management

Dear Parents,

Our system of classroom behavior management is simple. I would like to explain it to you here so that when you come into the classroom, you will easily be able to read and understand our color chart.

On a classroom chart, each student has a pocket in which five color cards are kept. This chart will make students aware of their behavior and help them to self-monitor. The colors and what they represent:

- ♦ **Green:** super citizen!

- ♦ **Yellow:** warning, improper behavior

- ♦ **Orange:** lose one recess; time-out to think about actions

- ♦ **Purple:** consequence of infraction to be decided by teacher (losing recess, trash detail, loss of a privilege, etc.)

- ♦ **Red:** parental contact to remedy situation

I keep a record chart showing each student's color at the end of the day. At the end of the week, any student showing only yellows will be rewarded. If the entire class has only yellows for 10 consecutive days, we will celebrate with a class party or video.

With this system, I reinforce positive behavior. If any student persists in negative behavior, his or her parent will be contacted. Please reinforce at home that each child is responsible for his or her own behavior. Self-discipline is one of the best lessons a child can learn!

Sincerely,

_____

Class Schedule

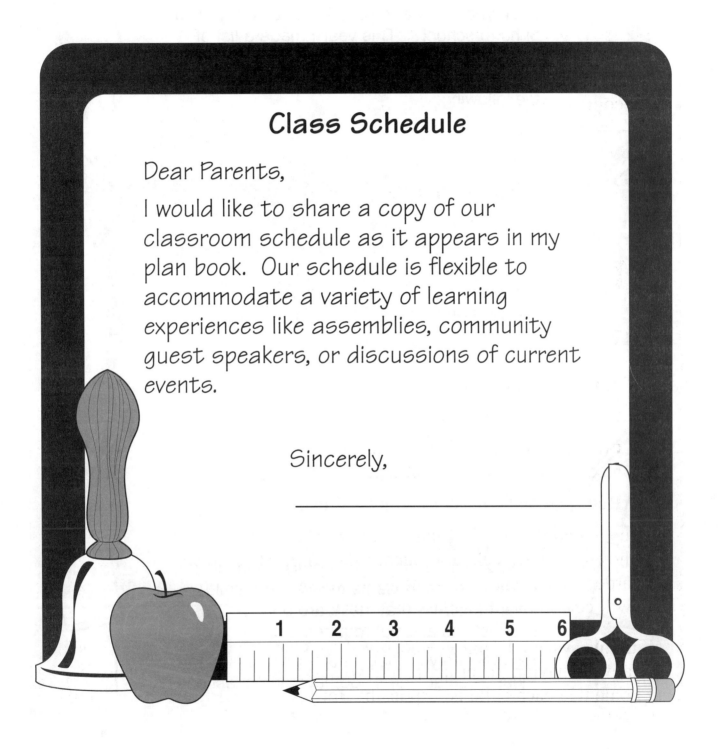

Class Schedule

Dear Parents,

I would like to share a copy of our classroom schedule as it appears in my plan book. Our schedule is flexible to accommodate a variety of learning experiences like assemblies, community guest speakers, or discussions of current events.

Sincerely,

_____

Student Supply List

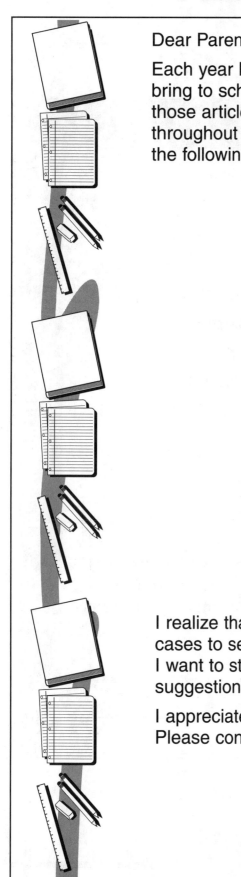

Dear Parents,

Each year I am asked, "What should my child bring to school?" This year I made a list of those articles that would be especially useful throughout the school year. These include the following:

I realize that it may not be possible in all cases to send those items with your child. I want to stress that these are only suggestions and not requirements.

I appreciate your help and continued support. Please contact me if you have any questions.

Sincerely,

_____

Homework Policy

Dear Parents,

Homework has a definite place in the educational process. It is an extension of the learning experience children have during the instructional day. Homework is designed to aid the student in achieving classroom and school goals, and it should never be used to punish or merely to keep students busy.

Students in my class will be assigned approximately _____ minutes of homework per day.

The homework I give falls into one of these four categories:

1. **Remedial Drill:** This is an extension of work that has been introduced in class. This homework is an individualized drill activity designed to help strengthen the child's weak areas.

2. **Research:** This is work which involves the use of reference materials. It is often given on an extended-time basis.

3. **Unfinished Work:** This is work that is not completed in class and is within the student's capability to finish at home.

4. **Review:** This is time spent at home studying and preparing for tests.

If your child is ill but able to do schoolwork at home, I will be happy to prepare assignments that can be done without direct teacher instruction. Please call the school by the start of the school day to make arrangements for work to be picked up that afternoon.

Sincerely,

_____

Home Study

Dear Parents,

Your help is needed in order for your child to have the best experience in completing homework. Students need to have something in which to carry their materials to and from school. At home, their folders or backpacks should be stored in the same place so that they are always handy and able to be located when needed. It is also a good idea for you to take a look in the backpack each day to determine if there have been any notices or papers sent home.

Good work habits begin at home. It will be useful to arrange a set time each evening for your child to complete his or her homework. It is also important to provide your child with the proper equipment in a well-lit, quiet area of your home. If the supplies are readily available, the work will be completed that much quicker.

Here is a list of supplies it may be worthwhile for you to keep on hand.

- sharp pencils and/or pens
- marking pens
- crayons
- ruler
- stapler
- hole punch
- transparent tape
- scissors
- construction paper
- notebook paper
- glue and/or paste
- colored pencils
- eraser

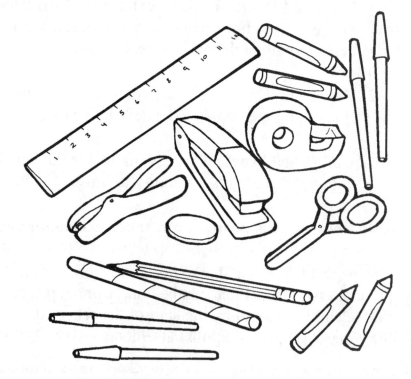

Set up a routine so that after homework is completed, your child puts it in the proper place so that it is ready in the morning. Help your child to take responsibility for the work. After all, it is his or her homework, not yours.

Thank you for your help and support.

Sincerely,

_____

Ways to Help at Home

Dear Parents,

I am often asked by parents how they can help to support their children's education at home. Here are some suggestions that may be of help to you.

❑ When booklets and papers are brought home, look at them, comment on them, and review them with your child. Show genuine interest in the work. This communicates the idea that education is important, and it encourages your child to do well in school.

❑ Talk with your child daily about school, everyday happenings, and current events.

❑ See that your child gets plenty of sleep. Encourage exercise and good nutrition.

❑ Monitor television programs. Television can be instructional and also relaxing in proper doses and at the proper times. Talk with your child about the programs he or she watches. Turn off the television during meals to facilitate conversation.

❑ Instruct your child to complete homework as early in the afternoon or evening as possible.

❑ Provide a quiet, well-lit area in which your child can study. Set up a desk or table designated for study but not far from the rest of the family. Remember to provide materials such as pens, pencils, a pencil sharpener, paper, a dictionary, crayons, glue, and scissors.

❑ Insist that homework be done away from the television and other distractions. Please be aware that some individuals work best with background music, but for others it is far too distracting. Get to know what works best for your child.

❑ Take an active interest in your child's schoolwork. Assist your child when he or she has an upcoming test and needs to study, even if that assistance is simply providing plenty of quiet time. It is also helpful to quiz your child orally on the information he or she is studying.

❑ If your child has trouble understanding something, try to help.

❑ Be aware of study strategies such as flash cards that can be shared with your child.

❑ Provide learning experiences outside of school. Parks, museums, libraries, zoos, historical sites, and family games offer good learning experiences.

❑ Encourage your child to write.

❑ Read with your child and around your child. Encourage your child to read for pleasure. Discuss what your child read, what you read together, and, where appropriate, what you are reading.

❑ I hope this information proves helpful to you. As always, I appreciate your support.

Cordially,

_____

Homework Packet

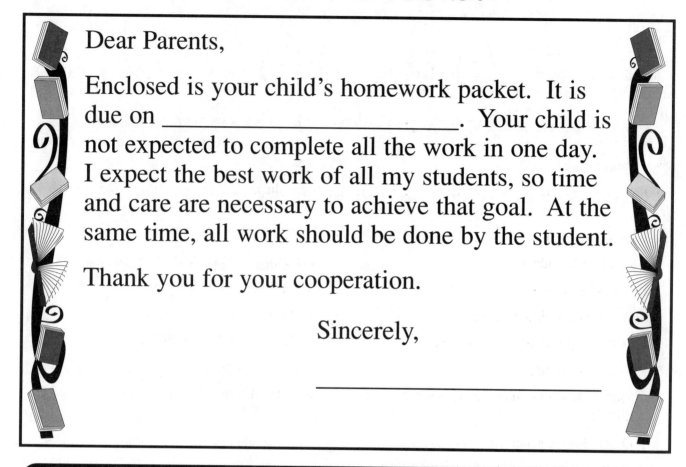

Dear Parents,

Enclosed is your child's homework packet. It is due on _____. Your child is not expected to complete all the work in one day. I expect the best work of all my students, so time and care are necessary to achieve that goal. At the same time, all work should be done by the student.

Thank you for your cooperation.

Sincerely,

_____

Date_____

Dear Parents,

Please help your child complete and correct the attached work and return it to school on _____. The time you spend will help your child get the most out of the assignment. Thank you for your cooperation.

Sincerely,

_____

108

Volunteers

Attention!
Volunteer Help Needed

Dear Parents,

Children need to have good role models and warm, loving adults around to work with them. If you have a little extra time and the desire, your help will be greatly appreciated.

Please mark the things below that you will be willing to do at school.

❏ Read with students.

❏ Check student work.

❏ Work on cooking projects.

❏ Teach physical education games.

❏ Help with centers.

❏ Prepare teaching materials (photocopy, cut, ditto, etc.)

❏ Help limited-English speaking students.

❏ Work in a computer lab.

❏ Help with art projects.

❏ Help with science projects.

❏ Help with music or dance.

❏ Help with theatrical productions.

❏ Other (Please specify.) _____

I can use the help of volunteers during the days and times listed below. Circle those that work best for you. I will notify you of any requirements for working in the classroom and when we will need to begin. (**Note:** If you would like to help but do not have the time during the school day, materials can be sent home with your child for you to prepare in the evening and send back to school the next day. Make a note on this form if you can be a home volunteer.)

Thank you in advance for your help.

Mondays	**Tuesdays**	**Wednesdays**	**Thursdays**	**Fridays**
Time	*Time*	*Time*	*Time*	*Time*

Sincerely,

_____

_____
Volunteer's Name

_____
Child's Name

Volunteers (cont.)

Help Wanted!

Moms   Dads   Grandparents

There are excellent part-time opportunities waiting for you in the classroom! We need the following:

- room moms/dads to plan games, entertainment, special crafts, and so forth for our class parties
- classroom help once a week to help with the students in one or more areas of the curriculum
- sharing of particular hobbies or expertise with the students

No experience necessary . . . just a little time to spare and to share. The work is rewarding and fun, and the environment is always exciting!

Contact_____

Guest Speakers

Dear Parents,

I have found that one of the best resources for enriching our classroom experiences are our very own parents. Many of you have interesting occupations and hobbies that your child would enjoy having you share with the class.

If you are willing to share your occupation or hobby with the class, please complete the section below and return this form with your child. I will contact you to arrange a time.

I appreciate your time and effort. Thank you for your assistance.

Sincerely,

_____

Name:_____ Occupation: _____

Hobbies: _____

Best day and time for me to speak to the class: _____

Guest Speakers

It is your child's turn to find an interesting and appropriate guest speaker to bring to class. The scheduled day and time is _____ at _____. (The time is flexible, if necessary.)

Your child must do the following:

1. Contact the speaker by letter or telephone.

2. Introduce the guest to the class.

3. Write the speaker a letter of thanks.

This page must be turned in the week before the speaker is scheduled.

Speaker:_____

Occupation:_____

Address: _____

Phone Number: _____

Why did you select this speaker? _____

_____

_____

Write your introduction for this speaker on the lines below._____

_____

_____

_____

_____

Independent Study

To the parent(s) or guardian(s) of _____,

I understand your child will be absent from school on the dates of _____ through _____. I feel confident that during this time you will want to provide meaningful tasks for your child to ensure continued learning success. Please have your child complete the following items:

❏ daily journal entries

❏ attached math pages

❏ reading in _____, pages _____ to _____

❏ mini report on the area or event you visited during your vacation

❏ map of your travel route

❏ reading of the daily newspaper and a discussion with you of current events

Your child may choose additional tasks if he or she wishes and turn them in upon your return. I look forward to seeing all of you back home safe and sound and to hearing about your many adventures.

Sincerely,

_____

Birthday Celebrations

Dear Parents,

Birthdays are special occasions, and we enjoy celebrating them at school. Please know that you are welcome to send treats to the classroom on your child's birthday, either of the edible or material kind. However, it is not necessary to send treats, and whether or not treats are present, we will be sure to take a few moments to honor your special birthday child.

Best wishes,

_____

Dear Parents,

Birthdays are special occasions, and we enjoy celebrating them at school. However, I would like to eliminate sugar treats on birthdays by suggesting each child "treat" our class to a book donated to the classroom library. A bookplate with your child's name will be placed inside the front cover. You are not obligated to do this, but I think it is a meaningful way for a child to share his or her birthday in a special way with the class. I am sure your child's favorite books are good choices, but feel free to ask me if you would like some book suggestions.

Summer and non-school day birthdays can also be celebrated! One idea for summer birthdays is to celebrate the mid-year mark. For example, if your child's birthday is July 24, why not celebrate it in school on January 24? Weekend and holiday birthdays can be celebrated on the nearest school day.

Best wishes,

_____

Explanatory Note for Progress Reports

Dear Parents,

As progress reports go home today, I would like to send you a few words of explanation. Our progress report was designed to give you an indication of your child's growing skills and maturity. I am always concerned when putting progress reports in writing that parents or children will try to determine the child's academic future. This report is meant merely as part of the ongoing communication between school and home in terms of the current progress. Many factors go into determining future potentials.

I also caution you against making comparisons of your child's report with those of your other children or your child's classmates. I have seen many children and parents hurt and discouraged when comparing, forgetting that the progress of one child can in no way compare to the progress of another. Everyone is an individual and evaluated as such.

If you wish to discuss this report and to gain additional feedback, please feel free to contact me to arrange a conference. I will be happy to discuss any of your questions or concerns.

As always, it is a pleasure to share in the education of your child.

Sincerely,

_____

Progress Report

Student: _____ **Teacher:** _____

Room: _____ **Date:** _____

This progress report tells you about your child's academic and social growth and development over the past _____ weeks. After reading this report, please fill in the form below. Return the bottom portion by _____.

Areas of growth: _____

_____

_____

_____

Areas to work on: _____

_____

_____

_____

Suggestions: _____

_____

_____

_____

_____
_____
Teacher

- -

Parent: _____ **Child:** _____

Comments: _____

_____

_____

I would like to arrange a conference time. Please contact me at _____.
phone number

Pre-Conference Letter I

To the parent(s) or guardian(s) of _____,

Our parent-teacher conference is scheduled for _____.
I am looking forward to meeting with you to discuss your child's progress.

In order for us to plan this conference, it is important that you express your areas of concern and interest. Please respond to the following items and return the bottom portion to me by _____. Your feedback is appreciated.

Thank you for your participation.

_____
Teacher

Name:_____

Child's Name:_____

☐ The scheduled conference time is acceptable.

☐ I am unable to attend at the scheduled time. Please call me at _____ to schedule another appointment.

☐ My child's attitude toward school is _____

_____

☐ My child's interests outside of school are _____

_____

☐ In order to understand my child better, you should know_____

_____

☐ Please circle three topics from those listed or write additional areas that you would like us to discuss during our conference time.

- homework
- self-discipline
- listening skills
- health
- friendships

- respect for authority
- general curriculum
- self-confidence
- working with a group
- other_____

Please write additional comments below or on the back of this paper.

_____

_____

Pre-Conference Letter II

Dear Parents,

Since the start of the school year, I have been getting to know your child, his or her interests, and how he or she learns. However, there is, of course, a great deal of time outside of school that I do not spend with your child, and certainly your perspective and experience of your child will vary to some degree from mine. In that light, I would appreciate reading your written perspective before we get together for our upcoming conference. Please take a few minutes to respond to the following questions and return them to me by _____.

Thank you for your assistance.

Sincerely,

_____

Name:_____   Date:_____

Child's Name:_____

- What are your child's feelings about school, both positive and negative?

  _____

  _____

- What do you see as your child's greatest personal assets?

  _____

  _____

- In what scholastic or other areas do you think your child needs to improve?

  _____

- Who are your child's current role models and heroes?

  _____

- What would you like to see happen for your child educationally over the next school term?

  _____

Pre-Conference Letter III

Dear Parents,

Student's Name_____

Our conference is scheduled for _____, _____
                                            day   date
at _____ in _____. At that time, we will
              time   place
discuss _____'s work habits, test results, homework, academic
                    student's name
progress, social skills, and special talents.

Please come prepared with any questions of your own. You may list them on the
response sheet below, if you wish. Please return the bottom section of this form
to me by _____.

I am looking forward to meeting with you.

                                                    Yours truly,

                                                    _____
                                                            Teacher

- -

Name:_____

Child's Name:_____

Teacher:_____

Scheduled Conference Date and Time:

☐ Yes, I will be able to meet at our scheduled time.

☐ No, I am unable to meet at the scheduled time. Please contact me at

_____ to arrange a different day and/or time.
      phone number

Some things I would like to discuss at our conference

include: _____

_____

                                                    _____
                                                          Parent signature

Conference Reminder and Cancellations

Dear _____,

Just to remind you, our conference is scheduled for _____
<small>time</small>

on _____. I look forward to meeting with you.
<small>date</small>

Sincerely,

_____

Dear _____,

Unfortunately, I must reschedule our upcoming conference due to unavoidable circumstances. I apologize for any inconvenience this causes you. I will call you to arrange a new conference time.

Thank you for understanding.

Sincerely,

_____

Dear _____,

I am sorry we missed seeing each other for our scheduled conference time. I am sure you were unavoidably detained. Perhaps you can let me know another day and time that will suit your schedule. I am sure you are as anxious to meet and discuss your child's progress as I am.

Sincerely,

_____

Supply Request I

Dear Parents,

We are beginning a new unit of study. As always, we will be doing a variety of activities around our theme. In order to make our experience a success, we are asking for the donation of special supplies that we will need during our course of study. If you have and would like to donate any of the following, please send them to school with your child by _____.

_____

_____

_____

_____

_____

_____

_____

_____

_____

_____

Thank you for your assistance.

Sincerely,

_____

Supply Request II

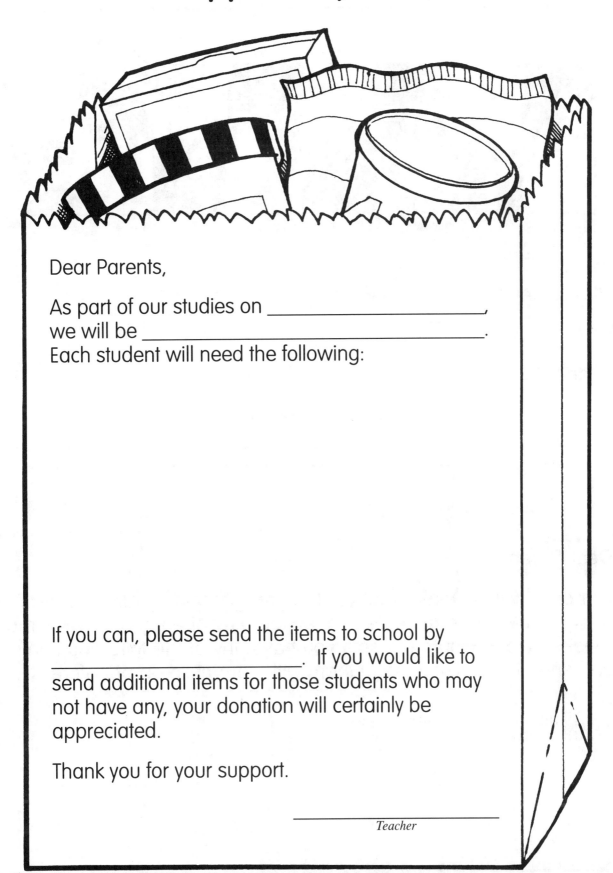

Dear Parents,

As part of our studies on _____,
we will be _____.
Each student will need the following:

If you can, please send the items to school by
_____. If you would like to
send additional items for those students who may
not have any, your donation will certainly be
appreciated.

Thank you for your support.

_____
Teacher

Request for Ingredients

Dear Parents,

Please help with our cooking project by sending_____

on or before _____.

Thank you.

The Gourmet Chefs of Room _____

Dear Parents,

Our class will be making lots of fun projects this month. Many of our activities will require items that you may already have at home. Please take a minute to see if you have any of the following items on hand. If so, please send them with your child on or before

_____.

Thank you.

_____
Teacher

Party Supply Request

Dear Parents,

Can you help us with our _____ party? If so, please send _____ on or before _____.

Thank you.

_____
Teacher

Dear Parents,

Our class is having a party to celebrate _____.
Please check any item you can send on or before _____ and return this form tomorrow.

Thank you for your assistance.

_____
Teacher

Name: _____

Child's Name: _____

Phone Number: _____

Share Time I

Dear Parents,

Your child's share time is scheduled for _____.

Sharing is a time for children to learn more about each other, to develop oral language skills, and to become comfortable speaking in front of a group. Anything of interest to your child will most likely be appropriate to share with the group.

Your help is requested in preparing your child for Share Time. Please help your child to choose something to share. Postcards or pictures are helpful if students wish to share about a family trip or event. Current events, especially if accompanied by a newspaper article and photograph, make good topics if the student is prepared and well informed. Games and puzzles are also good to share as long as the child is ready to tell the class how they work.

The key to good sharing is practice, practice, practice so that the speaker is comfortable and well rehearsed. Please help your child plan what to say and practice how to say it. Give plenty of praise and suggestions for improvement, if necessary.

If your child wishes to share a pet, please inform me ahead of time so arrangements can be made.

Thank you for taking the time to help prepare your child. Be sure anything your child brings to school is clearly marked with his or her name.

Sincerely,

_____

Share Time II

Dear Parents,

Your child's weekly/monthly share day is_____.
On this day, he or she will be asked to share something of
interest to him or her. These include but are not limited to
the following:

- books
- hobbies
- collections
- special toys
- trophies and awards
- talents

- simple activities or crafts
- word and mind puzzles
- information about a family trip or event*
- a pet**

Please help your child to prepare by practicing what he or
she will say and how. Give plenty of praise and suggestions
for improvement.

If your child is absent on his or her share day, we will
schedule a new day as time allows.

Thank you for your assistance.

_____
Teacher

*Photos and postcards are helpful here.

**Please inform me ahead of time so arrangements can be
made.

Teach and Tell

Dear Parents,

Your child's scheduled Teach and Tell will take place on _____.

Since preschool or kindergarten, your child has probably been participating in share time. Now he or she is ready for what we call Teach and Tell. This differs from simple sharing in that the child is responsible for teaching his or her classmates a simple activity or skill. Ideas include but are not limited to the following:

- a mind game

- a logic puzzle

- a craft such as origami

- words in a foreign language

- a "how to"

- the rules of a sport or game

- an anagram

- a science experiment

- a science fact

- a math fact

- explanation of how something works

The best place to begin when choosing a topic for Teach and Tell is with your child's particular interests and hobbies. Once the decision has been made, please help your child to prepare by watching him or her rehearse, offering praise, and suggesting improvements.

Thank you for taking the time to help your child prepare for Teach and Tell. The more rehearsal he or she has, the better the presentation is likely to be.

Sincerely,

_____

Halloween Party

Happy Halloween!

Dear Parents,

Our annual school-wide costume parade will take place on
_____ at _____. All students are
invited to come to school in costume; however, costumes are not
required. Parents are invited to attend, as well, to watch the
parade and to photograph the event. The adventurous can also
come in costume!

Please remember to send your child with regular school clothes so
he or she can change out of the costume after the parade. For
obvious safety reasons, please choose costumes that are
comfortable, easy to move in, and allow clear vision. Please note
that no weapons, fake blood, or gory costumes will be allowed.

Thank you.

_____
Teacher

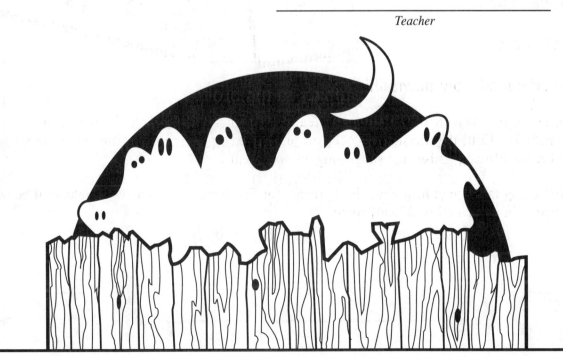

Winter Program

Dear Parents,

On _____ at _____, our school will host a winter holiday program. You and your family are invited to attend. During the program, our students will perform, and the bigger and friendlier the audience, the better.

Feel free to bring your video cameras to record the event. The winter program is always a crowd pleaser, and you will want to preserve the memories of your child's performance.

Please use the form below to let us know if you will attend our performance. We would like to have a good idea of the number who will be here so that we can plan refreshments. Return the form with your child by _____.

Thank you,

_____
Teacher

- -

Name:_____

Child's Name:_____

☐ Yes, we will be happy to attend this year's winter program. Number attending: _____

☐ No, unfortunately we will not be able to attend this year's program.

Newsletters

Newsletters are invaluable tools of communication between the classroom and home. A weekly newsletter is an excellent way to keep parents/guardians apprised of your units of study, special days, and future needs. Remember, too, to let parents know about future field trips, guest speakers, holiday news, birthdays, and so forth. If possible, it is a good idea to include anecdotal materials and samples of student work.

Publishing Your Newsletter

There are as many ways to publish a newsletter that you and your class can create. On the following pages are some newsletter forms that are simple and handy to use. There are also a variety of seasonal borders included on pages 205–215. Clip art of all kinds can be found on pages 216–224. (**Note:** The purchase of a clip art book or a clip art computer program is an excellent investment for any teacher.)

Working Together

An excellent way to build writing and communication skills is to work on the newsletter together. Enlarge a newsletter form, using an overhead or a sheet of butcher paper, and have the students dictate or fill in the information. This has the added benefit of re-emphasizing to them their current course of study and upcoming lessons and events. When preparing the newsletter, young children can be encouraged simply to report what is happening, while older students can write a bit of editorial to accompany the information. Students might also be allowed to draw the art to be included in your newsletter. Computer technology can go a long way in providing options for the look and the layout. Whatever you choose, let the students be a part of the newsletter. The learning that comes from this "real-life" application will be invaluable.

Newsletter Frame I

What's News?
by Room _____

Date:

Newsletter Frame II

The Class News

Week of_____

Feature of the Week

_____
_____
_____
_____
_____
_____
_____
_____

Monday	Tuesday	Wednesday	Thursday	Friday

Newsletter Frame III

Newsletter Frame IV

Field Trip

We're Going on a Field Trip!

Where: _____

When: _____

Why: _____

_____

How: _____

Please bring _____

_____

Please sign the permission slip below and have your child return it by _____. Your child will not be allowed to participate without the signed permission slip.

Thank you.

_____
Teacher

- -

My child, _____, has my permission to participate in a field trip to _____.

I understand that transportation to and from the field trip will be

❏ by school bus   ❏ by car

❏ on foot   ❏ other_____

_____   _____
date   *Parent signature*

❏ I will be happy to chaperone. Please contact me at_____.

daytime phone number

Unedited Student Writing

Dear Parents,

Attached you will find a sample of your child's writing. You will notice that it has not been corrected. Research shows that teacher or parent correction of grammar, spelling, handwriting, and sentence structure inhibits a child's initial self-expression. However, I want to assure you that my curriculum provides formal instruction in all areas mentioned. Writings such as the sample attached are meant primarily to foster the student's creativity and fluidity. Many such writing samples are then taken through the writing process wherein all corrections are made and the piece is polished to its best state.

Please enjoy your child's creative writing. Praise and enthusiasm will give your child more confidence to express him or herself creatively in the future.

Sincerely,

_____

Spelling Philosophy

Dear Parents,

Until now your child has often used "invented" spelling in much of his or her writing. Invented spelling is the formation of the written word according to the way it sounds to the child. It is a typical and natural way for emerging writers to begin shaping words. However, your child is now ready to begin looking carefully at the correct spelling of the words he or she uses.

With that in mind, we are beginning to study a set of spelling words each week. We will use the words during our lessons throughout the week, and homework will often involve them. The words can be a part of your home life as well. The following are suggested ways in which you can support your child's learning of the correct spelling for each word.

★ Together with your child, find the words in newspapers and magazines.

★ Play word games.

★ Write the words using different media (thick pens, markers, thin pens, sand, crayons, pencils, paint, makeup, etc.)

★ Do rainbow writing. The child forms the words using one color crayon. He or she then writes on top of the word in another color. Do this repeatedly for up to four or five colors.

★ Use magnetic letters on the refrigerator to spell the words.

★ Use cereal or macaroni letters to form the words.

All these methods are effective alternatives to traditional drills. The end result is the same without the corresponding drudgery.

As always, thank you for your support.

_____
Teacher

Bringing Home Books

Dear Parents,

Today your child is bringing home a little book. This is just one of many your child will receive this year. The little books are miniatures of the books, poems, or charts we are using in the classroom. Let your child read the book to you. Do not worry if your child does not know all the words or if he or she has merely memorized the text. This is how reading begins. Celebrate what your child can do and the interest shown in wanting to read. Thank you for taking the time to share these little books. Your involvement is critical to your child's success.

Sincerely,

_____

- -

Dear Parents,

I am bringing this book home to read to you. Please take time tonight to listen to me read it. Help me to remember to return it to school tomorrow.

Thank you.

_____

Television Tonight

Dear Parents,

We are currently studying _____
as a part of our unit on _____.
                         topic

The following television program,

_____,

will be shown on channel _____ on _____
                                      date

at _____.
   time

This program provides information which will help your child gain understanding of our current study. Your child will benefit from watching it (and you will enjoy it, too).

We will be discussing the program in class.

Thank you for your assistance.

Sincerely,

_____
Teacher

Reacting to Student Work

Dear Parents,

Today your child is bringing home some work for you to enjoy. You may find yourself thinking, "What can I say about this?" Here are some ideas.

- Tell me about this picture.

- These colors are exciting.

- Tell me why you chose these colors.

- This is an interesting story. Please read it to me.

- Where did you get these interesting ideas?

- I can tell you enjoyed doing this.

- This is something special.

- This is quite an accomplishment. How do you feel about it?

Open-ended questions and phrases such as those above are beneficial when discussing children's work with them. Such comments also help children to develop their own critical thinking skills.

Remember that your child's work is a creation of self-expression. Help your child to develop an appreciation of self and the unique quality of his or her own work by proudly displaying some of the pieces he or she creates.

Sincerely,

_____

Messy Day

WARNING!

We will be

_____
activity

_____
date

On _____
date

we will be _____
activity

Dress for Mess!

Science Fair

Dear Parents,

Our ability to solve present and future problems depends on our ability to question the world in new and creative ways. With our knowledge of the world growing so rapidly, we must move away from having our children simply memorize facts. Computers can do that much better and more efficiently. Instead, we must emphasize the thinking skills that can put those facts to use and create organization for new facts as they emerge.

What better opportunity for a child to develop such skills than to participate in our school's science fair! The thinking skills a child develops while doing a science project are the same basic skills that will be used throughout life—to sense and clarify problems that exist and to find creative solutions to those problems.

Please encourage your child to take part in this year's science fair. Children should select projects that match their interests and abilities. The science fair experience should be fun for your child—something he or she really wants to do.

You will find an attached list of ideas as a springboard for you and your child's imagination. Be creative, be investigative, and most importantly, have fun!

Sincerely,

_____

Science Fair Ideas—Level 1

1. How much salt does it take to float an egg?	21. Do bigger seeds produce bigger plants?
2. What kind of juice cleans pennies best?	22. Which materials absorb the most water?
3. Which dish soap makes the most bubbles?	23. Do wheels reduce friction?
4. Do watches keep time the same?	24. What materials dissolve in water?
5. On which surface can a snail move faster—dirt or cement?	25. What is the soil in my schoolyard made of?
6. What brand of raisin cereal has the most raisins?	26. Does holding a mirror in front of a fish change what the fish does?
7. How can you measure the strength of a magnet?	27. What color of birdseed do birds like best?
8. Do ants like cheese or sugar better?	28. What holds two boards together better—a nail or a screw?
9. Can the design of a paper airplane make it fly farther?	29. Will bananas brown faster on the counter or in the refrigerator?
10. Do the roots of a plant always grow downward?	30. Does temperature affect the growth of plants?
11. Can you tell what something is just by touching it?	31. Do mint leaves repel ants?
12. What kinds of things do magnets attract?	32. Does a ball roll farther on grass or dirt?
13. What foods do mealworms prefer?	33. Do all objects fall to the ground at the same speed?
14. How long will it take a teaspoon of food dye to color a glass of still water?	34. Does anyone in my class have the same fingerprints?
15. Does a bath take less water than a shower?	35. Which travels faster—a snail or a worm?
16. Can you tell where sound comes from when you are blindfolded?	36. Which paper towel is the strongest?
17. Can plants grow without soil?	37. Can plants grow from leaves?
18. Does warm water freeze faster than cool water?	38. Which dissolves better in water—salt or baking soda?
19. In my class who is taller—the boys or the girls?	39. Can things be identified by just their odors?
20. Do different types of apples have the same number of seeds?	40. With which type of battery do toys run longest?

Science Fair Ideas—Level 2

1. How far does a snail travel in one minute?	21. Does the color of water affect its evaporation?
2. Do different types of soil hold different amounts of water?	22. Can you separate salt from water by freezing?
3. Will adding bleach to the water of a plant reduce fungus growth?	23. How does omitting an ingredient affect the taste of a cookie?
4. Does water with salt boil faster than plain water?	24. Do suction cups stick equally well to different surfaces?
5. How far can a person lean without falling?	25. Which student in class has the greatest lung capacity?
6. Can you tell time without a watch or a clock?	26. How much weight can a growing plant support?
7. How far can a water balloon be tossed to someone before it breaks?	27. Will water with salt evaporate faster than water without salt?
8. Does the shape of a kite affect its flight?	28. Does it matter in which direction seeds are planted?
9. Does an ice cube melt faster in air or water?	29. Which cheese grows mold the fastest?
10. Does sugar prolong the life of cut flowers?	30. Do all colors fade at the same rate?
11. How much of an orange is water?	31. Which brand of diaper holds the most water?
12. Which liquid has the highest viscosity?	32. In my class, who has the smallest hands—the boys or the girls?
13. Will more air inside a basketball make it bounce higher?	33. Which kind of cleaner removes ink stains best?
14. Does the color of light affect plant growth?	34. Does a plant grow bigger if watered by milk or water?
15. Does baking soda lower the temperature of water?	35. Which brand of soap makes the most suds?
16. Which brand of popcorn pops the most kernels?	36. Does a baseball go farther when hit by a wooden or metal bat?
17. Which brand of popcorn pops fastest?	37. Do living plants give off moisture?
18. How much can a caterpillar eat in one day?	38. Using a lever, can one student lift another student who is bigger?
19. In my class, who has the biggest feet—the boys or the girls?	39. Which gets warmer—sand or dirt?
20. Do plants grow bigger in soil or water?	40. What kind of glue holds two boards together better?

Science Fair Ideas—Level 3

1. What type of line carries sound waves best?	21. Which way does the wind blow most frequently?
2. Can the sun's energy be used to clean water?	22. Does the size of a light bulb affect its energy use?
3. Does a green plant add oxygen to its environment?	23. For how long a distance can speech be transmitted through a tube?
4. Which metal conducts heat best?	24. Which grows mold faster—moist bread or dry bread?
5. What percentage of corn seeds in a package will germinate?	25. What type of soil filters water best?
6. Does an earthworm react to light and darkness?	26. Does the color of a material affect its absorption of heat?
7. Does the human tongue have definite areas for certain tastes?	27. Does sound travel best through solids, liquids, or gases?
8. Can same-type balloons withstand the same amount of pressure?	28. Do sugar crystals grow faster in tap water or distilled water?
9. Does the viscosity of a liquid affect its boiling point?	29. Can you see better if you limit the light that gets to your eye?
10. Does surrounding color affect an insect's eating habits?	30. How much of an apple is water?
11. Do children's heart rates increase as they get older?	31. What common liquids are acid, base, or neutral?
12. Can you use a strand of human hair to measure air moisture?	32. Do taller people run faster than shorter people?
13. What materials provide the best insulation?	33. Does the length of a vibrating object affect sound?
14. Is using two eyes to judge distance more accurate than using one eye?	34. Does a plant need some darkness to grow?
15. Do different kinds of caterpillars eat different amounts of food?	35. Who can balance better on the balls of their feet—boys or girls?
16. What plant foods contain starch?	36. Does exercise affect heart rate?
17. What keeps things colder—plastic wrap or aluminum foil?	37. Which dish soap makes the longest lasting suds?
18. Does heart rate increase with increasing sound volume?	38. What are the effects of chlorine on plant growth?
19. Do boys or girls have a higher resting heart rate?	39. Which type of oil has the greatest density?
20. Do liquids cool as they evaporate?	40. How accurately can people judge temperatures?

Overdue Work

To the Parent or Guardian of _____ ,

The following assignments are overdue and must be completed by _____ in order to receive credit.

_____

_____

_____

_____

_____

_____

_____

_____

_____

_____

_____

_____

In order to promote habits of completion and satisfaction for a job well done, please have your child complete the assignments immediately and return them to me. Attach this note signed by you with the completed work.

Thank you.

_____
Teacher

_____   _____
Parent   *date*

Back-to-School Night Invitation

IT'S BACK-TO-SCHOOL NIGHT AND YOU ARE INVITED!

Date:

Time:

Room:

Back-to-School Night is an opportunity for parents to meet with their child's teacher and to learn more about the curriculum, activities, and events of the coming year. Your attendance is most welcome and appreciated.

See you there!

Open House Invitation

Directions: Cut out the pieces along the dotted lines. Glue the top pattern to the bottom pattern where shown.

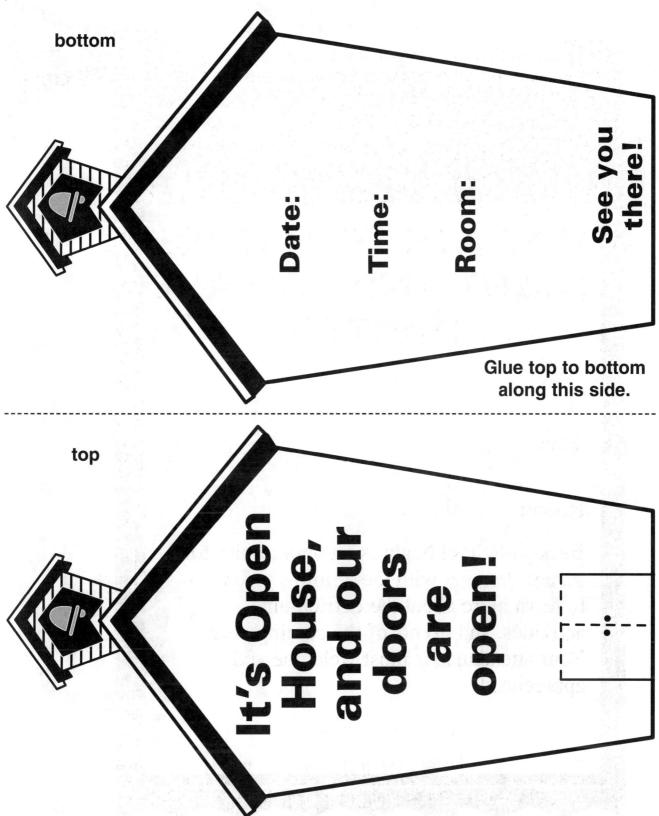

bottom

Date:

Time:

Room:

See you there!

Glue top to bottom along this side.

top

It's Open House, and our doors are open!

General Invitation

YOU ARE INVITED!

Where:

When:

Who:

Why:

Please let us know if
you can make it.

General Information

A Flyer for Parents!

Stay Tuned!

Business Letter Outline

_____
your address

_____
city   state   zip

_____
date

_____
organization

_____
address

_____
city   state   zip

_____:
greeting

_____

_____

_____

_____

_____

_____
closing

_____
signature

Request for Information

Use this format when sending a letter to a book publisher, member of Congress, etc., or requesting field trip information. It is best to use official school stationery. If you do not have school stationery, use the letter format below.

School Address

Dear _____ *,*

The students in _____ *at* _____
are very interested in learning more about _____ .

We would appreciate any information you could send us.

> *Yours truly,*

This is a request to an author accompanied by students' letters.

School Address

Author's Address

Dear _____ *,*

As you can see by the enclosed letters from my students, they are enjoying your books tremendously. We have been studying the writing process, and they became authors themselves. They have many questions for a published author whose works they enjoy. The most often asked questions seem to be When did you write your first story? and Where do you get your ideas?

We anxiously wait for your reply.

> *Sincerely,*

Field Trip Inquiry

Write this letter on school stationery. Otherwise, follow the format on this page.

Date

School Address

Addressee

Dear_____,

I am a teacher at_____ in

the_____District.

My_____class is learning

about_____.

A field trip to_____would be a great

experience to enhance their learning.

Please send me information concerning the cost, what a tour of
the facility would include, how much time the tour would take,
and the dates and times available.

Please send any additional brochures or application forms.

Thank you.

Sincerely,

_____

Teacher Note: *Always send information about the field trip site to chaperoning parents ahead of time along with information about what is expected of them as a chaperone. This will help your field trip experience to run smoothly.*

Parental Assistance for Field Trips

Dear Parents,

We need parent volunteers to accompany us as chaperones on our field trip to

_____ on

_____. We will leave school at

_____ and return at _____.

If you would like to help, please sign and return the section below.

Thank you for your assistance.

_____
Teacher

Yes, I would like to attend as a chaperone on your upcoming field trip.

Name: _____

Child's name: _____

Daytime phone number:_____

SCHOOL BUS

Parental Assistance in the Classroom

WANTED!
HELPING HANDS

Date: _____

Time: _____

Activity: _____

Please return the bottom section with your signature if you can help with this activity.

Thank you for your assistance.

_____
Teacher

- -

Yes, I would be happy to help with your upcoming activity.

Name: _____

Child's name: _____

Daytime phone number: _____

Change in Student Behavior

Dear_____,

I am writing this letter out of concern for _____.
I have noticed a definite change in_____'s
performance in class, and I was hoping you might have
some insight to share with me. I am sure if we pool our
resources, we can make this a positive and productive
year for _____. Please let me know a
convenient day and time we can meet. My phone
number at school is_____.

Sincerely,

_____

Student Progress

Name_____ Date_____

Effort	Work Habits	Behavior
____ Outstanding	____ Works Independently	____ Is a Leader
____ Very Good	____ Needs some guidance to complete assignments	____ Sets a Good Example
____ Good	____ Needs constant guidance to complete assignments	____ Is Improving
____ Needs to improve	____ Easily Distracted	____ Forgets Self Control
	____ Distracts Others	

____ If checked here, please sign and return.

_____ _____
Teacher signature *Parent signature*

Note of Condolence

Transfer these notes to personal stationery.

Dear_____,

I was saddened yesterday to learn of_____'s death. Please accept my condolences.
<small>name</small>

I want to reassure you that during this time I will keep a watchful eye on_____. I will lend any support
<small>student's name</small>
I feel is necessary.

If I can be of any help to you,_____, please let
<small>name</small>
me know.

Sincerely yours,

_____

Dear_____,

I am terribly sorry to hear about the hardship your family is going through at the present time.

I hope the situation will be remedied soon. In the meantime, I want to reassure you that I will be supportive at school for your_____, _____.
<small>son/daughter</small> <small>name</small>

Sincerely,

_____

Letter of Recommendation for Student Teacher or Aide

Transfer this letter onto school stationery.

Date

To Whom It May Concern:

It has been my pleasure to have worked with
_____ during the _____
semester of the _____ school year.

_____ is committed to excellence in
teaching. He or she has set very high standards for
him/herself and has worked continuously to meet his
or her goals. He or she has added a new dimension
to _____ by bringing _____.
He or she is also extremely energetic, witty, and
intelligent which has endeared him or her to other
staff members. He or she is well liked by students
and respected by their parents.

I highly recommend _____ as an
outstanding educator. He or she is extremely
competent in the areas of classroom management,
planning, and instruction. _____ will
be a valuable asset to any school staff.

Sincerely,

_____

Letter of Limited Recommendation

This letter is designed for a person who, at the present time, is not as prepared as he or she should be, but who shows promise for the future. Transfer this letter onto school stationery.

Date

To Whom It May Concern:

I have supervised _____ during the _____ school year. _____ brings enthusiasm to the classroom.

_____ is extremely energetic and with time and maturity will learn to channel that energy into productive ways to enrich his or her classroom.

_____ is well liked by students, and communication with parents is an area that will, no doubt, be enhanced through experience.

_____ will be a nice addition to your staff and will complement a veteran teacher in a team-teaching situation.

Sincerely,

_____

Congratulations and Appreciation

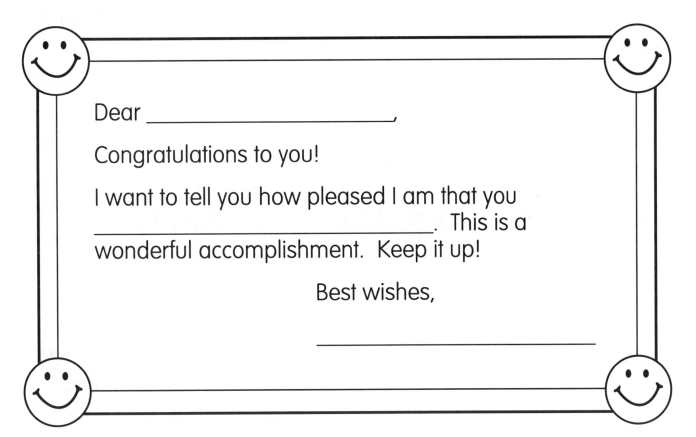

Dear _____,

Congratulations to you!

I want to tell you how pleased I am that you
_____. This is a
wonderful accomplishment. Keep it up!

Best wishes,

_____

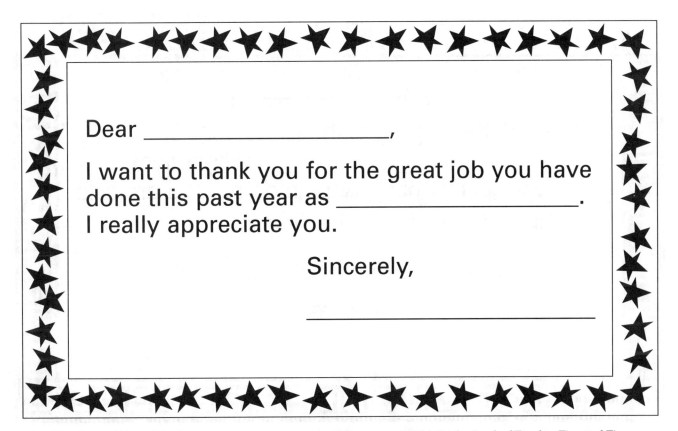

Dear _____,

I want to thank you for the great job you have
done this past year as _____.
I really appreciate you.

Sincerely,

_____

Thank You for Helping

Dear _____,

Thank you for helping us on our field trip to _____. It is people like you who make special learning experiences possible.

Sincerely,

_____

Dear _____,

Thank you for helping in the classroom on _____. Without your help, we would not be able to do special projects like this.

We hope you will work with us again soon.

Sincerely,

_____

Certificate of Achievement

This is to certify that

_____,

parent of

_____,

made a difference in the life of a child.

This parent's involvement in education has made our school a better place.

With thanks and appreciation,

_____
Teacher

_____
Date

Terrific!

Participation

Parent

Volunteer Thank You

Dear_____,

I want to take this opportunity to express my most sincere thanks for taking the time to _____ _____.

In this day of busy schedules, it is especially gratifying to see individuals such as yourself giving freely of your time in assisting schools in meeting their educational goals for students.

I want to especially mention

_____.

Thanks for your help. Have an enjoyable and relaxing summer.

Cordially,

_____

Outstanding Volunteer Award

This certifies that

_____

has been an outstanding volunteer in our room during this school year!

Thank you for your special dedication!

Outstanding
Volunteer

_____
Teacher

_____
Principal

_____
Date

Goodbye to Kindergarten Parents

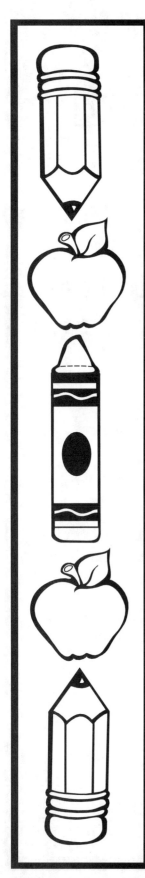

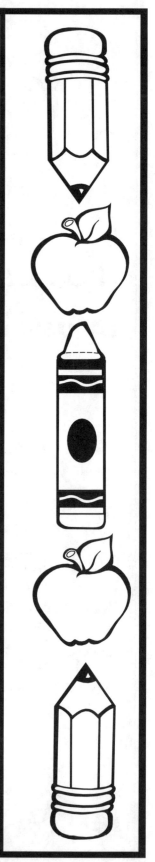

Dear Parents,

I could not let the school year draw to a close without a comment on what I think was a very special class. Happy, well-adjusted children tend to come from caring homes. Your positive attitudes toward your children's education have been reflected in their enthusiasm and willingness to learn.

I have appreciated your support in so many ways.

- Our wonderful parent volunteers have given their time and given of themselves to make our program work.

- Those of you who couldn't volunteer your time have been so generous in sending things to help us in our program. Thank you very much.

- We have had wonderful parties this year thanks to our very efficient and very well-organized room parents.

Recently, I had a talk with the class about first grade. I told them how they would be split up in different classes and have different teachers. There was a moment of silence—a flicker of dismay crossed their faces—and then came the smiles, "Oh boy! We get to eat lunch in school! We will read! We will write our own stories!" I was so proud of them. They have that magnificent self-confidence that makes them eager to reach out for the new challenge. This is what school and life are all about. They are great! They are ready! They are your children!

Sincerely,

_____

Parent Goodbye

Dear Parents,

This has been a productive and interesting year in your child's education. I have enjoyed the part I've been able to play in contributing new ideas and experiences. Your child's eagerness and willingness to learn are a reflection of the importance you place on education.

I have appreciated your support in so many ways.

Wonderful parent volunteers gave of their time and themselves to make the program work.

Those of you who could not volunteer your time have been so supportive and generous in sending things in to help our program. A big thank you! Your behind-the-scenes support is crucial, too.

Our fun parties this year have in large part been organized by our room parents. Many others have also contributed; thanks to all of you.

Next year will be a big step for your child, appropriate for his or her capabilities. You can do much this summer to make next year an even better one. Be positive about your child's placement. Encourage your child to accept responsibility.

Help your child learn to make decisions and accept the results of those decisions. Give your child the gift of organization and a strategy to develop it. Share times that are creative, not necessarily expensive. Encourage independence, but do not expect it to be absolute. Have fun!

I am very proud of the progress that your child has made. I will enjoy watching them reach out for challenges and the future. That is what school and life are about.

My best to all of you.

Sincerely,

_____

Goodbye Certificate

It was a

PLEASURE

having

_____

in my class this year!

_____
Teacher

_____
Date

Summer Suggestions

Dear Parents,

Because your child will be out of school for a significant period of time during the summer, I would like to offer some suggestions for continued practice of reading and writing skills.

Gifts That Promote Reading and Writing

- Books, both fiction and nonfiction (includes cookbooks, craft books, biographies, etc.)
- Magazine subscriptions
- Models that have written directions for assembling

Reading Activities

- Reading newspaper and magazine articles
- Reading recipes and cooking foods

Writing Activities

- Sending a card or letter to someone far away
- Writing family shopping lists (for groceries, presents, etc.)

Memorizing Activities

- Story retelling
- Songs

Games That Require Reading

- Trivia games
- Spelling/Vocabulary games
- Board games

Reading and Writing Activities Using the Newspaper

- Cut out words that belong to word families we have studied.
- Collect interesting pictures. Be ready to explain what they are about.
- Learn a new word every day. Tell what section of the newspaper it came from.
- Collect interesting news items.
- Read "Dear Abby" and try to think of other ways to solve the writer's problems.
- Collect interesting cartoons, and draw one of your own.
- If your newspaper has a puzzle page for students, try to work the puzzle.
- Look in the classified ad section. Find a job you would like to have. Try to figure out what the abbreviations in the ad stand for.
- Design a newspaper ad for your favorite consumer item.
- Pretend you have made an amazing discovery or invention. Write a newspaper article about yourself.

Other Ideas to Try

- Play a twenty questions game.
- Compare and contrast items at a store.
- Explain all the different things you can do with a variety of objects.
- Games that require reading
- Diaries
- Reading directions for making gifts
- Reading street signs and maps
- Writing thank-you letters for gifts
- Poems
- Plays
- Crossword puzzles
- Word searches
- Dictate a story to a friend or relative.
- Write clues for a treasure hunt.

Happy vacation! Happy reading!

Sincerely,

Student Vacation

Dear Student,

You have been working very hard and doing a good job with reading and writing in the last few weeks. I am pleased with your progress.

The time has come for a little vacation. I hope you will find some interesting things to do during that time. Be sure to tell your mom and dad that you will be available to do some work around the house!

Do not forget about reading and writing! Here are some good ideas for reading and writing activities using the newspaper:

1. Cut out words that belong to word families you have studied.

2. Collect interesting pictures. Be ready to explain what they are about.

3. Learn a new word every day. Tell what section of the newspaper it came from.

4. Collect interesting new items.

5. Read "Dear Abby" and try to think of other ways to solve the writer's problems.

6. Collect interesting cartoons and draw one of your own.

7. If your newspaper has a puzzle page for students, try to work the puzzle.

8. Look in the classified ad section. Find a job you would like to have. Try to figure out what the abbreviations in the ad stand for.

9. Design a newspaper ad for your favorite consumer item.

10. Pretend you have made an amazing discovery or invention. Write a newspaper article about yourself.

Happy vacation! Happy reading!

_____

Introductory Letter to Students
(Primary)

Dear _____,

Student's name

Welcome to the _____ grade! I am glad you are a part of our class. We will be sharing an exciting year together, learning about _____

_____

_____

_____

I cannot wait to discover what interests you have to share with the class.

Welcome aboard!

_____

Teacher

Grade

Introductory Letter to Students
(Intermediate)

Welcome!

I am happy to welcome you to my class this year. I am looking forward to an exciting year as we share our ideas, talents, and interests.

We will make our class rules together as a class. Please begin brainstorming on the paper provided when you finish reading this letter.

This year we will be learning _____

_____

_____

_____

_____

_____

_____

_____

Please feel free to tell me about any special interests or knowledge that you have. We will always be happy to explore interesting new topics as the year progresses.

If you ever have any questions or concerns, do not hesitate to bring them to my attention. All problems can be solved with openness and teamwork.

Here's to a wonderful school year!

_____
Teacher

Student Greeting

_____ Date

_____ Teacher

is part of our class team this year. Welcome!

Class Guidelines

Teacher Note: Adapt these guidelines to meet your own classroom needs. The following guides are only suggestions.

Welcome to Our Class

Our new year is under way, and I am so glad you will be a part of it.

In order to make the year run smoothly, there are some guidelines that we all need to follow. Keep these guidelines with you. They are important for you to know.

- Treat everyone with courtesy and respect.

- When the teacher or a classmate is sharing, do not interrupt.

- Do not use the teacher's or another student's supplies without asking permission.

- Listen carefully to all instructions.

- Complete all assignments neatly and on time.

Everyone is expected to know and follow these rules. If we all do so, we are sure to have a wonderful, exciting school year.

Nameplates

Teacher Note: Affix these nameplates to each student's desk or table at the start of the new year to help you and the students get to know one another.

Nameplates *(cont.)*

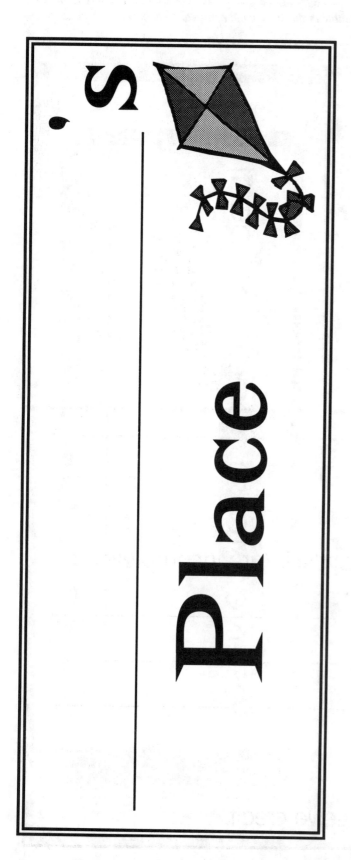

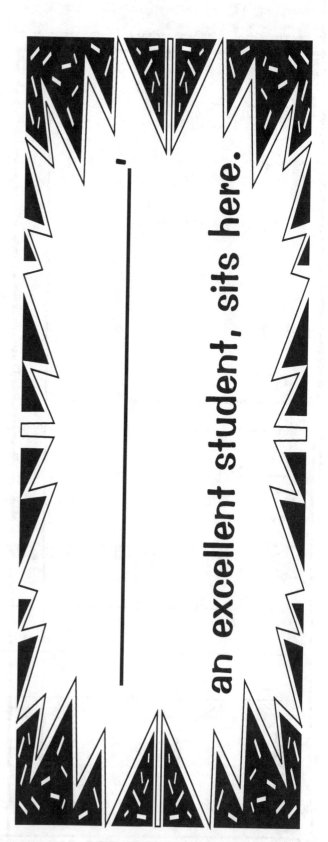

Incomplete Work

Whoops! Something is missing!

Please complete

by _____.

Just a Reminder!

Incomplete Work

The following assignment(s) is/are incomplete:

_____

_____

_____

_____

It/They must be completed by _____ in
order to receive credit.

Missing Work

MISSING

_____'s Work

Room _____ reports that the following assignment is missing:

_____

_____

If found, please return it immediately to the proper authorities.

Missing Assignments

The following assignments are missing from my record book:

_____

_____

_____

If you have forgotten to turn them in, please do so now. If you have never finished them, please see me today to make a plan for completing them.

Completed Work

Fantastic News!

This is to report that _____

has successfully completed all homework assignments

from _____ **to** _____

Please let your parents know about your good work.

Congratulations!

_____
Teacher

_____
Date

Appreciation Certificates

Thanks for the helping hand!

I couldn't have done it without you!

_____
Teacher

_____
Date

Thank you, _____,

from the bottom of my heart.

_____
Teacher

_____
Date

Terrific Tickets

Teacher Note: *Pass these out to students anytime you see them doing something particularly helpful or kind such as helping a classmate or showing exceptional courtesy on the playground. Offer prizes such as erasers, stickers, or free time when a student redeems five tickets.*

Terrific Ticket

I caught you being terrific!

Terrific Ticket

I caught you being terrific!

Terrific Ticket

I caught you being terrific!

Terrific Ticket

I caught you being terrific!

Terrific Ticket

I caught you being terrific!

Terrific Ticket

I caught you being terrific!

Terrific Ticket

I caught you being terrific!

Terrific Ticket

I caught you being terrific!

Thank You for Gift

Dear_____,

Thank you for

_____.

You were very thoughtful to remember me in such a way.

Enjoy your vacation!

Thank you.

Dear_____,

This has been such a special year because I've had thoughtful students like you in my class. I really appreciate the gift of

_____.

Thank you very much.

Dear_____,

I really appreciate the _____. I'm sure to use it often, and when I do I will think of you.

Thank you.

Dear_____,

Thank you for _____ taking the time to remember me by making

_____. It was very dear of you to think of me.

Thank you.

184

Birthdays 1

Hip-Hip-Hooray!

You're _____

today!

Happy Birthday from

_____

Happy birthday to you.

Happy birthday to you.

Happy birthday, dear

_____,

Happy birthday to you!

Birthdays II

Happy _____th Birthday

Happy Birthday to You!

_____ is
name

_____ years old!
age

Missing Tooth

Another one for the Tooth Fairy?

Congratulations,

_____!

from _____

(What do you think she does with all those teeth anyway?)

Tiiiiiiimmmmm-berrrrrrrr!

There goes another one!

Congratulations, _____!

from _____

Hooray for Me!

Teacher Note: Duplicate these awards and give them to students as they reach various milestones. One is blank to complete with your own message.

Hooray for Me! *(cont.)*

Hooray for me!

I know how to tell time.

Hooray for me!

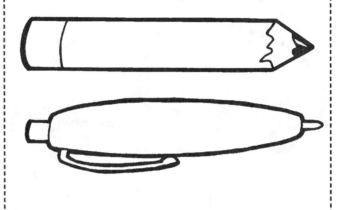

I know how to write in cursive.

Hooray for me!

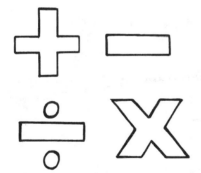

I know how to

_____ add   _____ subtract

_____ multiply   _____ divide

Hooray for me!

Treasure Chest

Teacher Note: Use this and the following pages for student incentives. Give each student the base piece (in this case, the treasure chest) to begin, labeled with his or her name. If desired, display the bases on a bulletin board with an appropriate title (such as "Worth Their Weight in Gold" for this incentive). Using whatever criteria you decide, give each student a filler or attaching piece each time it is warranted. Add a filler piece to the base each time one is earned. You might also offer a reward after so many pieces. For example, anyone earning 10 gold coins receives 15 minutes of free time or gets to take home the class pet for a night.

Ice-Cream Cone

Train

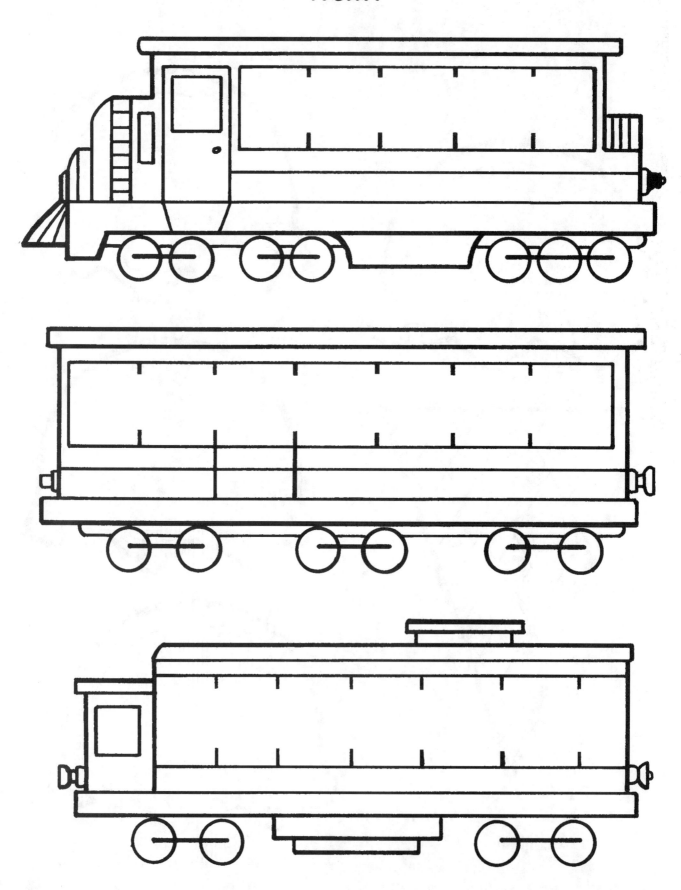

Candy Jar

Warm Fuzzies

It is often a good idea to recognize students for their little successes each day. Use these and the following reward cards to offer a "warm fuzzy" to any student of whom you are proud.

Seasonal Warm Fuzzies

Vonderful!

Gobble, Gobble, Good

Super star

Sweets to the Sweet

You're a Treasure!

Somebunny Special

Get Well Notes

196

Bookmarks

Teacher Note: Offer these to students in reward for good work or behavior.

Kindergarten Graduation

Congratulations!

You have graduated from kindergarten.

Good job!

Teacher

Principal

Date

Grade Advancement

Congratulations, _____ !

You are now a _____ grader.

Good work!

_____
Teacher

_____
Principal

_____
Date

Advancement Certificate

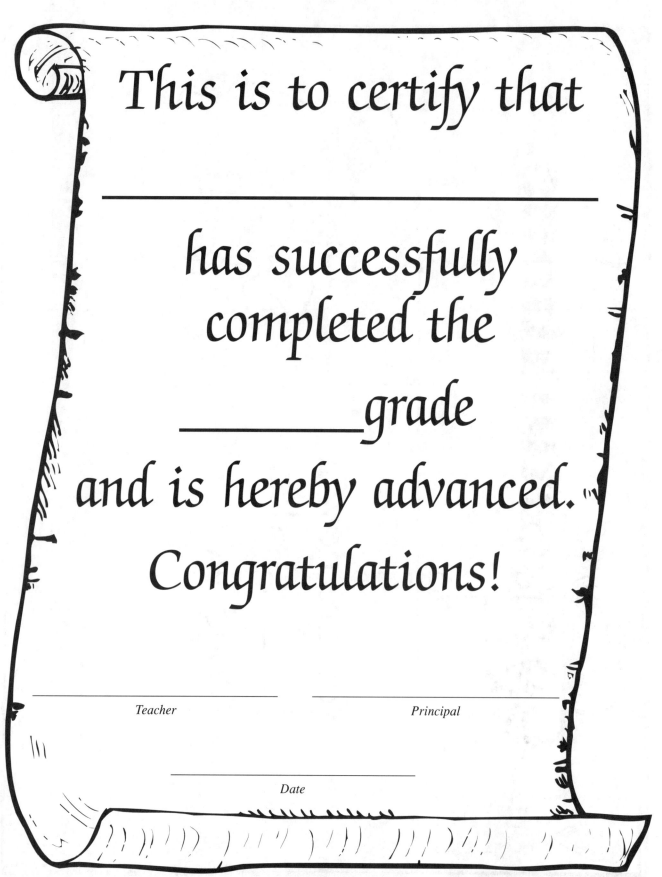

This is to certify that

_____

has successfully completed the

_____ grade

and is hereby advanced.

Congratulations!

_____   _____
Teacher   Principal

_____
Date

Goodbye Letter (Primary)

Dear _____,

I have been so glad to have you in my class this year. Your smile, curiosity, and hard work made my days extra special. Thank you for being you!

Good luck next year as a _____grader!

Yours truly,

_____

Goodbye Letter (Intermediate)

Dear _____,

This past year has been one of adventure and learning for me. I hope it has been the same for you.

I cannot tell you what a pleasure it has been to have you in my class this year. I have enjoyed watching you learn and grow from a quiet, young _____ grader to the mature, confident child you are today. Please know how proud I am of you.

I wish you all the best in your years of education to come. Always remember what you have learned here and all you have achieved. You have a right to be proud. Good luck!

Best wishes,

_____

Farewell Certificate

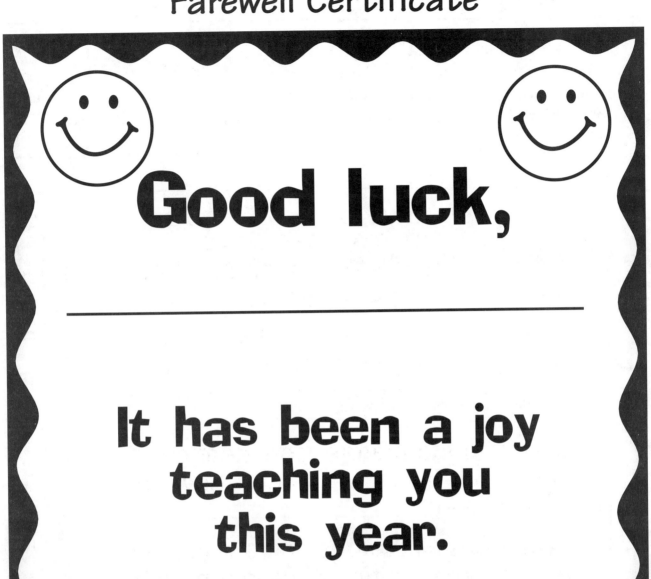

Good luck,

_____

It has been a joy teaching you this year.

_____
Teacher

_____
Date

Teacher Note: When the year is over, give this form to the students so they can assess the year for themselves. Keep a copy for yourself—it will prove very enlightening for you!

What I Have Learned This Year

- We did so many things this year, it is hard to remember them all. What things do you remember most about this past year?

  _____

  _____

  _____

- What are some things you learned this year that really stand out for you?

  _____

  _____

  _____

- What is something you are proud to have learned this year?

  _____

  _____

  _____

- What did you like best about this class?

  _____

  _____

  _____

- How could this class be better?

  _____

  _____

  _____

Seasonal Borders: Back to School

Use this and the following borders to add seasonal touches to your communications.

Seasonal Borders: Fall

Seasonal Borders: Halloween

Seasonal Borders: Thanksgiving

Seasonal Borders: Winter

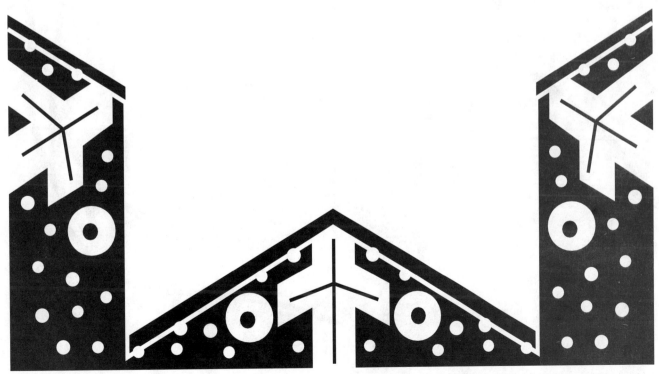

Seasonal Borders: Christmas

Seasonal Borders: Patriotic

Seasonal Borders: Valentine's Day

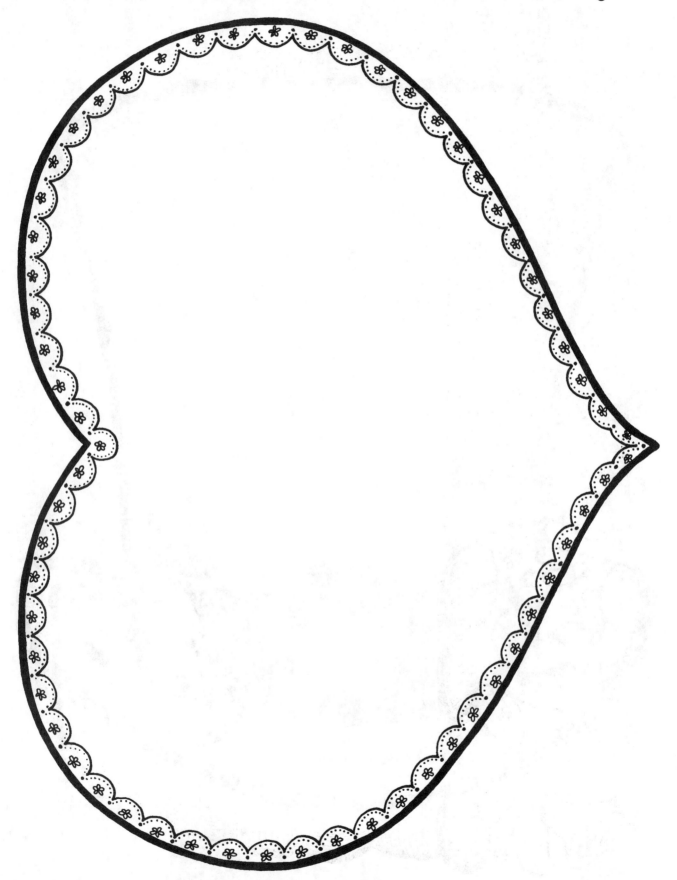

Seasonal Borders: Spring

Seasonal Borders: Easter

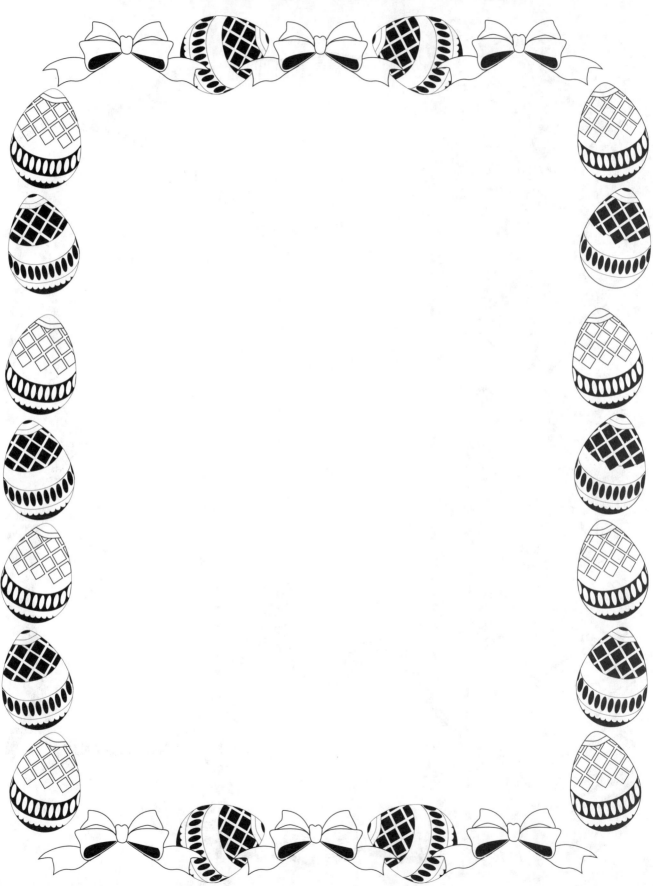

Seasonal Borders: Summer

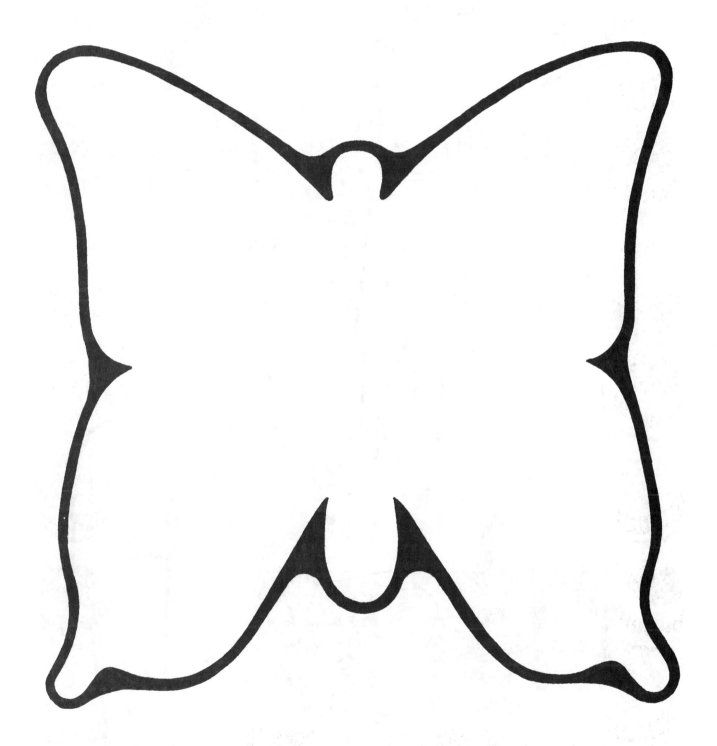

Clip Art

Use the clip art here and on the following pages to add special touches to your correspondence and worksheets. A little bit of art adds a lot of interest.

Clip Art (cont.)

Clip Art (cont.)

Clip Art (cont.)

Clip Art (cont.)

Clip Art *(cont.)*

Clip Art *(cont.)*

Clip Art (cont.)

Clip Art *(cont.)*

Student Assessment

There are many ways to assess the growth and competency of your students. The following pages list and describe a variety of techniques and provide supporting forms to utilize them in your classroom.

✤ Observation

Observation, when it is done really well, allows for immediate intervention. Small groups can be called together for instant mini-lessons on important concepts. Partners can be refocused on the task at hand. An individual student can be guided in the right direction with none of the wasted time that goes with the teacher's finding a mistake on the paper, circling it in red, passing it back, and hoping that the student will look at it before stuffing it into a backpack or worse, into the wastepaper basket.

Recording this kind of observation can become a major problem, however. Many experts recommend anecdotal records. Others have good things to say about checklists and other kinds of forms. Some teachers carry notebooks or cards on clipboards. Others just try to remember everything until after school and then make notes to drop into portfolios. Teachers who are lucky enough to have classroom aides depend on them to make notes. Whatever the system, the observation must be recorded, or it cannot become part of the assessment.

✤ Conferencing

Conferencing is another part of assessment. Conferences can be formal or informal, planned or spur-of-the-moment. The teacher uses this time to review and to analyze what the student has been doing and to help plan and implement the next steps in the student's learning.

Recording the results of a conference is much easier, of course, than recording observations. The teacher can be prepared with a form or some other system, and the student can help with the process. Moreover, the student's perspective is also considered, giving the conference somewhat greater scope than the observation.

✤ The Writing Process

The writing process makes up an important part of effective assessment. The multiple drafts that result from this process of self-editing, peer editing, teacher editing, revising, and polishing provide a ready-made record of student progress. (See page 348 for more information about the writing process.)

✤ Self-Evaluation

Journal entries, reading records, checklists, completed questionnaires, and the students' written reflections on their own work are also useful in tracking a student's progress. They are part of the self-evaluation aspect of assessment in which students are asked to rate their own progress and to take ownership of and responsibility for the process as well as the results.

Student Assessment *(cont.)*

✤ Paper-and-Pencil Tests

Traditional paper-and-pencil tests are still popular forms of assessment, even though experts warn that they can be artificial and limiting. Teachers are encouraged to make these tests as relevant to the actual activity of the classroom as they possibly can. Open-ended questions can be constructed, together with appropriate scoring rubrics, so that the assessment reflects what the students are really doing.

✤ Standardized Tests

Traditional paper-and-pencil tests also perform the function of getting students ready for the district-mandated, standardized tests. Even though many experts agree that the results of standardized testing are not meaningful or relevant and provide a limited or even false picture of what students are learning, standardized testing is alive and well within nearly every school district, and the public consistently uses the results as a barometer of student and school success.

A great deal is being written about helping both teachers and students to cope with the pressures of this kind of testing. It is interesting to note that there is a strong movement to create some kind of national standardized test at the same time as many educators are questioning the validity of this kind of testing at all.

There is, of course, no difficulty in recording the results of paper-and-pencil or standardized testing. The teacher simply places the corrected test or score sheet (or a photo copy) in the student's assessment portfolio. (See page 236 for more on portfolios.) The simplicity of the recording process and the clarity of the results are likely what perpetuate the use of this kind of assessment.

✤ Requirements

In summary, the best assessment requires authenticity, relevance, and the concentrated involvement of both teacher and student. Some incremental parts of the process are observation, conferencing, the use of the writing process, and self-evaluation, as well as traditional paper-and-pencil tests and standardized testing.

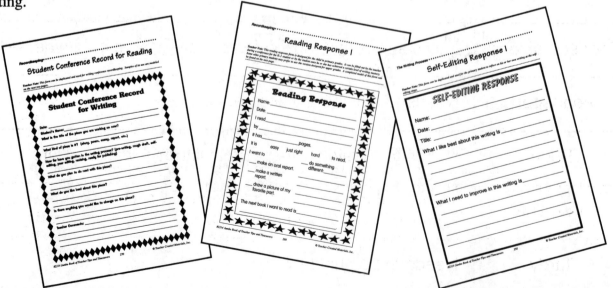

How Can I Say It?

Sometimes the trickiest part of assessment is figuring the best way to say something clearly but diplomatically. Here is a list of negative behaviors followed by appropriate euphemisms.

Behavior	Euphemism
Babyish	Is showing signs of immature behavior
Bully	Does not get along well with other children
Cheats	Needs help in learning to follow rules; Needs to do his or her own work
Disliked by other children	Often plays alone
Grade level too difficult	Depends upon others to help him/her
Inattentive	Spends much time daydreaming
Lazy	Needs to take the initiative and get right to work
Lies	Has trouble distinguishing reality from fantasy; Needs to be honest with classmates
Loud	Needs to develop a quiet voice for the classroom
Poor self-esteem	Lacks self-confidence; Seems to be unsure of him/herself
Poor sport	Needs to develop a sense of fair play
Rude	Needs to develop a respectful attitude towards others
Talkative	Talking more than listening; Needs to develop good listening skills; Would rather talk to friends than listen
Tardy	Needs to be punctual

Report Card Comments

Here and on the next six pages are a variety of comments you can use to help complete your report cards each term. It is sometimes difficult to find the words you need. These will help you.

Language Arts

- Speaks very well before the class
- Is showing good growth in basic skills
- Reading has improved considerably.
- Strongest work is in the area of creative writing
- Has shown an increased interest in_____
- Is trying hard and continues to make steady progress in _____
- Oral reading is fluent, and comprehension is good.
- Is making progress in all areas, especially in_____
- Is rapidly mastering the fundamental skills
- Is developing a fine vocabulary
- Is improving in reading, especially vocabulary development
- Enjoys the stories we read and participates in classroom discussions
- Applies skills to all written work
- Is an enthusiastic worker during the reading period
- Writes imaginative and creative stories
- Asks thought-provoking questions
- Uses imagination
- Strives to be accurate

- Explains himself/herself clearly
- Deduces meaning from information given
- Creates new ideas
- Originates ideas
- Communicates with accuracy
- Compares and contrasts similar and dissimilar things
- Is choosing suitably challenging reading material
- Is able to retell stories in correct sequence
- Is reading with expression
- Is working on the editing process
- Is able to self-correct

Report Card Comments (cont.)

Language Arts (cont.)

- Is able to identify the first and last part of a story

- Is able to recognize capital and lowercase letters

- Is able to listen to stories at the listening post while following the text in a book

- Is an eager reader during silent reading time

- Is making good use of our resource library

- Is using text and pictures to predict and confirm

- Has turned in extra-credit work

- Elects to read/look at books during "free choice" time

- Chooses to write during "free choice" time

- Is eager to take home books from our library

- Is eager to share his or her written work with the class

- Is making good progress recognizing high-frequency words

- Enjoys writing _____

- Oral reports demonstrate knowledge and research skills.

- Confidence and competence are increasing in _____.

- Is using approximations for spelling, which is very appropriate at this time

- Is beginning to use beginning and ending sounds to identify words

- Is beginning to use vowel sounds in writing words

- Is spelling many difficult words

- Is writing on a variety of topics

- Is writing in a variety of styles: friendly letter, factual reports, imaginative retelling, poetry, fiction

- Is enthusiastic about his or her personal journal writing

- Is doing a good job of dividing a story into paragraphs

- Is beginning to use the editing skills of placing periods, capitals, quotation marks, commas, question marks, and apostrophes

- Is eager to write

- Is eager to speak in front of a group

Report Card Comments (cont.)

Language Arts (cont.)

- Is becoming aware of some conventional spellings
- Uses expansive vocabulary
- Is using complex sentences in his or her writing
- Experiments with different styles in writing
- Is making good use of correct grammar
- Handwriting is a joy to read
- Handwriting is very legible
- Handwriting is very easy to read
- Makes an effort to make his or her handwriting legible
- Is learning to do independent research
- Is very successful in note-taking
- Is a major contributor at our brainstorming sessions
- Listens as well as shares during our discussions and presentations
- Is a good audience as well as presenter during our sharing presentation time
- Is able to analyze character actions
- Is able to analyze story plots
- Is able to compare books to others by same author
- Has many interesting story ideas
- Has well-developed characters in his or her stories
- Appears to have a good attitude about books
- Knows sounds of initial blends
- Knows sounds of final blends
- Is using initial blends in writing
- Is using final blends in writing
- Is using suffixes correctly: s, es, ing, ed, ly
- Is using prefixes correctly: pre, be, dis, re, post, un, in
- Uses a wide vocabulary in his or her writing
- Is beginning to use the dictionary
- Is competent using the dictionary

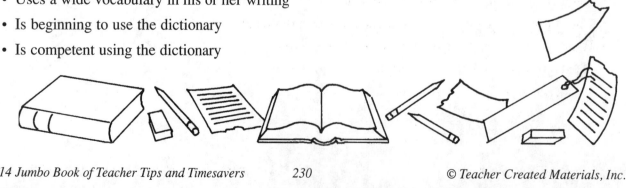

230

Report Card Comments (cont.)

Language Arts (cont.)

On those occasions when you need to convey less than positive information on report cards about language arts, the following comments will provide assistance.

- Showing some attention to print, but mostly making up meanings from pictures
- Is having trouble with recognizing letters of the alphabet
- Is just beginning to associate sounds with letters
- Has trouble sitting while listening to a story
- Is reluctant to speak in front of the group
- Is easily discouraged when_____
- Is hesitant to read his or her stories to the class
- Wants to talk instead of listening to others share ideas
- Still making many reversals (of letters, words, phrases)
- Has a limited vocabulary
- Doesn't seem to enjoy books or stories
- Lacks a good sight vocabulary
- Speech development may be hindering correct spelling.
- Reluctant to use approximation with word spelling, wants to be correct
- Is unable to retell a story with much accuracy
- Skims quickly through books without attention to detail
- Unable to predict story outcomes with confidence
- Is having a lot of difficulty with high-frequency words
- Is not using our classroom library
- Does not choose books or writing as an activity for free time
- Does not edit work carefully
- Unwilling to rework (rewrite or make changes) in written work
- Is capable but not willing to write or speak in front of class
- Is not making use of a dictionary or resource books
- Does not know how to use a dictionary despite repeated instruction
- Written work lacks description/details/varied vocabulary
- Has underdeveloped ideas in his or her writing
- Needs to slow his or her pace to be neater in his or her writing.
- Could improve his or her written papers with more attention to detail.
- Handwriting indicates that student is inclined to hurry
- Needs to focus on rules of grammar
- Unable or unwilling to write in daily journal

Report Card Comments *(cont.)*

Math and Science

In writing comments for student report cards, use the following phrases to make positive comments regarding students' progress in math and science.

- Is mastering math concepts easily
- Math/Science is a favorite area of study for_____.
- Has a naturally investigative nature
- Has a natural sense of order and organization that fosters understanding of math
- Is interested in science and collections
- Shares many interesting science projects from home
- Continues to turn in topnotch math assignments
- Particularly enjoys hands-on science experiments
- Strongest work is in science/math
- Is using the scientific method to investigate on his or her own
- Chooses to work on challenging math problems
- Is drawn to our science corner in all his or her free time
- Enjoys math manipulatives and can generally be found involved with them during free time
- Understands the one-to-one concept
- Is quite proficient with sorting and classifying
- Has grasped the difficult concept of long division/place value/fractions/decimals

On those occasions when you need to convey less than positive information on report cards about math and science, the following comments will provide assistance.

- Is having trouble with_____ (Review at home would be helpful.)
- Lack of attention in class may account for the difficulty he/she has with assignments
- It would help_____'s speed in arithmetic if he/she spent time each day on the multiplication facts.
- Needs to to study every evening. (Begin with_____.)
- Needs to review_____as he or she is having a great deal of difficulty
- Progress in_____is not consistent; review may be helpful.
- Does not understand the basic math concepts required in this grade (I would like to conference with you as soon as possible.)
- Seems to show no interest in our science program

Report Card Comments (cont.)

Fine Arts

In writing comments for student report cards use the following phrases to make positive comments regarding students' progress in fine arts.

- Shows good art expression
- Has a wonderful (creative) way of using color/design/concept
- Is very clever with pastels/clay/oils/paint/chalk
- Has a flair for art
- Has a creative mind that lends itself to great art expression
- Use of color is very interesting.
- Has an eye for detail
- Is willing to take risks with new art materials
- Is able to put on paper what other people can only imagine
- It is a joy to watch_____'s talents bloom (develop).
- Is an effective communicator, which is evident in his or her speeches
- Uses his or her voice to its best advantage with range and volume
- Clever wit makes his or her impromptu speeches most enjoyable.
- It is a pleasure to watch_____develop a character on stage.
- Has poise and grace on the stage
- Excels with his or her improvisation/pantomime/oral interpretation
- Handles dialogue with ease
- Creates a moving piece of artwork with his or her dancing
- Dancing is graceful and flowing.
- Enjoys our music time and joins in singing enthusiastically
- Likes to accompany our songs with rhythm instruments
- Enjoys acting out stories and poems
- Was a "star" addition to our classroom play
- Has a good ear for tune/pitch

On those occasions when you need to convey less than positive information on report cards about fine arts, the following comments will be of assistance.

- Is shy about speaking in front of the class
- Should experiment with new mediums of art
- Needs to show respect for different types of music
- Should spend more time practicing before performing
- Is shy about showing art to classmates
- Doesn't seem to enjoy class art projects
- Needs encouragement about his or her creativity
- Doesn't seem to take art seriously

Report Card Comments (cont.)

General

In writing comments for student report cards, use the following phrases to make positive general comments.

- Always knows answer when called upon

- Has qualities of leadership

- Well-liked by his or her peers

- Good sense of humor

- Shows respect for authority

- Has a good self-concept

- Works well in a group

- Is polite, kind, and well-mannered

- Makes an effort to learn

- Participates well in organized games on the playground

- Is an independent, self-motivated worker

On those occasions when you need to convey less than positive information on report cards, the following comments will provide assistance.

- Has qualities of leadership but...

- Needs to build self-esteem

- Needs constant encouragement

- Lacks interest in work

- Daydreams time away

- Hurries through work and makes careless mistakes

- Is capable of doing classroom work but rarely turns in assignments

- Assignments are not turned in or are very late.

Comments for School Records

Comments for School Records

Like the report card comments, these comments can be used to help you make notations on school records.

- Parents are cooperative and always willing to assist student with schoolwork.

- Parents attend all conferences and school functions.

- Parents provide enriching activities.

- Parents are interested in all areas of the child's education.

- _____is a valuable resource person willing to share_____.

- _____as our (room mother and/or library clerk) was a morning aide once a week.

- _____are eager to help and understand_____'s problems.

- Parents were divorced or separated this year.

- Parents want to help but find it difficult to be consistent.

- Parents have set unrealistic goals for_____.

- Single-parent family; child lives with_____.

- Parents work and are unable to help student at home.

- Parents have not responded to conference letters or phone calls home.

- It is helpful to have a translator in_____for conferences.

All About Portfolios

Portfolios have many functions from showcasing to assessment. A teacher may decide to have only one kind or all of them at once. Some of them belong to the student, some to the teacher, and some are jointly owned. In the process of starting somewhere, a teacher may change from one method to another, and it is important to remember that the portfolio process is not etched in stone. It is perfectly all right to try different approaches before finding the one that is most comfortable and productive for all concerned. None of them is right for everyone, and their names are not important. Different educators call them by different names.

This and the following pages outline several "how-tos" and "what abouts" concerning portfolios.

The Collection Portfolio

A collection portfolio is simply a folder that holds an accumulation of a student's work. Everything goes in it. It is what teachers used to call a "drop file."

The Showcase Portfolio

Artists, photographers, writers, actors, and models have always used portfolios to display and present either their work or some concrete proof of their talents and what they have accomplished. This showcase function of "real life" portfolios is also an important function of the classroom portfolio. One does not put everything into a portfolio. One selects according to some practical criteria such as "best work" or "shows growth" or "demonstrates completion of project." The work may represent one curricular area or many. The showcase portfolio is especially useful at conference times and open house nights.

Teacher/Student Assessment Portfolio

This is a collection of documentation, including copies of the work in a student's showcase portfolio, tests and test scores, anecdotal records of observations and conferences, and anything else the teacher may need to document an assessment of the student's progress and support that student's eventual grade.

Portfolio assessment, unless it is mandated and its components outlined are by the teacher's district, is pretty much what the teacher wants it to be. Its usefulness and credibility depend upon the expertise and professionalism of the individual classroom teacher.

Teacher Resource Portfolio

This is a file of general background material selected and saved to provide philosophical support to the teacher. It may include articles from professional journals, notes from educational classes or in-service meetings, references to books with relevant chapters, and so on.

How It's Done

Whatever portfolio system or systems you choose, formalize them by making labeled folders or boxes for each student. Stand them in a file box where everyone can get to them. This will cut down your work rather than add to it because the students can file their own papers in the folders. You can also add another job to the "Helper Chart"—Portfolio Monitor. This is someone who takes the responsibility of keeping the files in order. (Take a minute to explain or to reinforce alphabetical order by last name, and you will have accomplished another goal and provided practice time for each student as his or her turn arrives.)

There is one absolutely essential rule for this part of the process: All papers must be dated. This will make the eventual selection process easier and much more meaningful for evaluation purposes. The Portfolio Monitor can also double-check to be sure the papers are dated.

The Container

The container for the contents, the physical shape and size of the portfolio, can vary from the simplest piece of folded construction paper to a sturdy cardboard box for each student. Anything bigger would probably not be practical. How the teacher decides to house the contents of portfolios depends a great deal on the amount of room available. Since portfolios are supposed to enrich classroom life, these decisions should be made to promote ease and efficiency and should not make anyone's life more difficult. Experts stress only two requirements for these containers: they should hold what you want to put in them, and they should be easily accessible to teacher and student alike.

Decide on the Curricular Area

Deciding on the curricular area is the responsibility of the teacher, but there are no established rules. Most teachers, however, find that it is easier to begin this process with one area of the curriculum and then to add others as time goes by and the comfort level increases. Language arts is often a good place to start because the writing process is made to order for the portfolio, but if the teacher feels more comfortable with math, science, or social studies, those areas will work, too. In a classroom where themes are being used, a thematic portfolio might be appropriate. Decide on the limits for the portfolio and send the rest of the papers home.

How It's Done *(cont.)*

Selecting the Showcase Samples

Selecting the samples to include in the showcase portfolio is a decision the teacher and students should share. There are no hard and fast rules for this either. The teacher can guide the student by specifying the number of samples to choose, by asking for a certain number of samples from the beginning of the school year and a certain number of more recent samples (thus the importance of dates!), and by expressing a preference for certain pieces. The student, however, should be allowed to include those pieces of work that he or she feels are best or most important. Most educators agree that this kind of portfolio belongs to the student. The recognition of the student's "ownership" of both the papers and the underlying learning is crucial to the success of this approach. Self-evaluation is an integral part of this selection process. As the student selects samples for the showcase portfolio, he or she should be asked to "reflect" by using student-generated forms or writing his or her own. These reflections should be attached to the appropriate samples and included in the portfolio. It is also appropriate to ask the students to reflect on their progress over the year or a part of the year. The teacher may choose to respond to these reflections in writing. If so, these responses can also be included.

A showcase portfolio may contain a "folder within a folder" to accommodate things that are important to a student's self-esteem. These things can be associated with out-of-school activities such as sports, music, art, and drama as well as extracurricular, in-school activities such as student government. Research indicates that including things that are important to a student's life makes a better connection between school and the "real world." This is important to all students but may be especially important to students who are just learning English or who come from a different culture.

Select the Teacher/Student Assessment Samples

At this point, the teacher should make copies of the pieces that the student has chosen and put them in a teacher/student assessment portfolio. (The student's personal self-esteem folder should not be duplicated here.) You may already have this kind of file for saving test scores, anecdotal records, and the like. The teacher can also add other things to this portfolio, such as papers that the student did not choose but that you feel are meaningful.

A number of teachers who are dedicated to authenticity are providing an opportunity for students to evaluate their teachers. This can be done as a "quick write" or as a response to a structured evaluation form. The responses can be real eye-openers to teachers and be of help in planning classroom teaching strategies as well as in taking a look at management styles. This is not a technique recommended for the faint of heart, however, and must be carefully introduced and implemented. The results of such an evaluation can be kept in the teacher/student portfolio.

A New Kind of Organization

Most of this process, as you can see, is simply a different kind of organization, one that gives the student more input and makes assessment more authentic, more relevant to real learning. It may feel time consuming at first. That is why it is wise to go slowly, add one piece at a time, and stop when you reach your (temporary) limit without guilt or self-reproach. Adding even the first step of this process to your classroom will have an amazing positive impact on your effectiveness as a teacher.

What to Include

Ideas for the Collection Portfolio

- Introductory note to potential audience (parents, guests, interested educators, etc.)
- Writing samples—a writing process "package" showing an assignment taken from pre-writing through the editing and revision processes to the final, polished draft
    - writing samples showing different parts of the process
    - writing prompts and rubrics associated with samples
    - writing done for content areas such as social studies or science
    - writing inventory or checklist
    - writing samples reflecting different genres
    - journal entries
- Reading inventories or checklists
- Responses to reading
- Tape recordings of oral reading
- Photographs of projects and activities
- Videotapes of skits, activities, etc.
- Mathematics checklist and mathematics problem-solving samples

Ideas for the Showcase Portfolio

- Selection of items from the collection portfolio, showing the student's best work and growth over time
- Student's reflections on selections or general progress
- Self-esteem folder, including memorabilia, newspaper clippings, team photos, awards, snapshots, playbills, etc.

Ideas for the Teacher/Student Assessment Portfolio

- Photocopies of material from the showcase portfolio
- Anecdotal records
- Conference records
- Interest inventories
- Teacher-made tests and scores
- Standardized test scores
- Student evaluation of teacher

Ideas for the Teacher Resource Portfolio

- References to passages in books
- Student evaluation of teacher
- Articles from educational magazines and journals
- Notes from education classes and in-services
- Copies of administrative evaluations
- Notes from peer coaching

What to Include (cont.)

Suggested Content for the Showcase Portfolio

Sample A

2 quick-writes
2 journal entries
1 complete writing process package
1 peer editing response
1 reflection on the writing process
1 reading log
1 writing log

Sample B

1 complete writing process package from the first school month, including peer editing and reflection
1 complete writing process package from the second school month, including peer editing and reflection
1 reading log
1 writing log

Sample C

5 genre samples:
 • story
 • poem
 • descriptive essay
 • evaluation essay
 • biography
2 reflections on two of the above pieces
1 response to reading

Sample D

4 examples from the writing domain
 • evaluation
 • autobiographical incident
 • observational writing
 • firsthand biography
 • problem solution
 • report of information
 • speculation about causes
 • story
4 reflections of writing

Sample E

1 writing sample from each thematic unit:
 • animals
 • seasons
 • holidays
 • insects
2 quick-writes
1 reading log
1 writing log

Sample F

1 reading log
1 writing log
2 journal entries
2 writing samples from the beginning of the year
2 writing samples from the middle of the year
2 writing samples from the end of the year
1 reflection on progress

What to Include *(cont.)*

More About Math Content

Mathematically powerful students are those who use math to achieve their purposes and then communicate the results. They achieve their purposes in a variety of ways. They are comfortable with various thinking methods: they can analyze, predict, and verify; they can think about dimension and quantity; they can cope with uncertainty and change. They are well-equipped with the techniques and tools of math: they can calculate and compute; they can use concrete materials, diagrams, models, and mathematical notations.

They communicate their results though traditional mathematical means—numbers, symbols, graphs, and tables—but more and more they are being encouraged to communicate their results through language, both oral and written.

These communications—which may take the form of individual projects, math journals, decryption of difficulties and/or successes, as well as essays reflecting on progress and growth—are perfect materials for inclusion in a portfolio and a valuable tool in the assessment process.

More About Science Content

A written record of the scientific method in action is also material that is made-to-order for inclusion in the portfolio. The steps lend themselves to almost any grade level and provide student-generated products that will demonstrate growth and progress over a period of time.

- State the problem.

- Gather information.

- State your hypothesis. (*Make an educated guess.*)

- Investigate. (*Test your hypothesis.*)

- Draw a conclusion. (*Interpret data.*)

- Communicate results. (*Record on a graph or chart.*)

Flow Chart

This chart provides a good, at-a-glance overview of all the previous information on portfolios. Keep it in a useful place to help remind you of the flow.

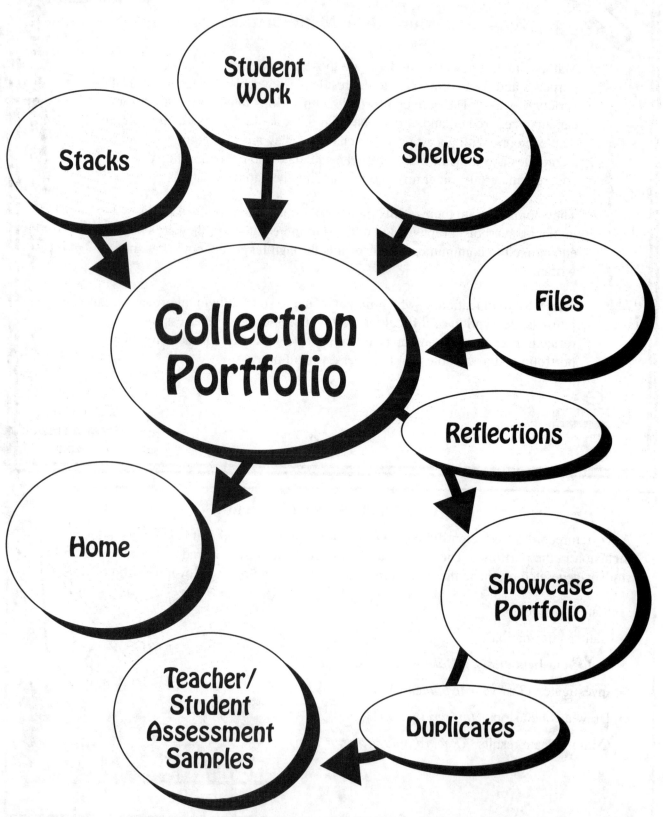

Using Portfolios for Assessment

So you have taken the plunge, saved and sorted what seem like millions of papers, written enough anecdotal records to make a best seller, conferenced with students, and checked the checklists. Now what? How do you use portfolio assessment?

If You Stopped with the Collection Portfolio

If you have decided the collection portfolio is your limit for the time being, then you can use it as an overview. You can browse through it before making an assessment of a student's progress. If the papers in the portfolio were dated, you can get a fairly good sense of the progress the student has made over a period of time.

If you would like to show the portfolio to parents at conference time, you may wish to organize it a little at first (or have the student organize it). The organization activity may actually ease you into the stage of the showcase portfolio, especially if the student does it. Most students are appalled by the quality of the work they did at the beginning of the year and want to make sure that their best efforts will be shown to their parents. At any rate, parents will be amazed at the amount of work that has been accomplished and can probably be persuaded to take it home with them so that you can start over. Save one or two of the very first papers so you can compare them with work done at the end of the year. Just leave them right in the folder. If they were dated, you will be able to find them again when you want them.

It is helpful to prepare and include a statement of your purpose in collecting these samples. Place it in the front of the portfolio so parents can glance at it at once. This kind of statement is also helpful when guests in your classroom (administrators, other teachers, aides, visiting students, and parents) pick up and glance through a portfolio. It is important to share this statement with the students. They also need to know the purpose behind saving these papers, and it is always nice if teachers and students are able to communicate the same information to interested parties. (There is nothing worse than having students act as if they had never seen their portfolios before!)

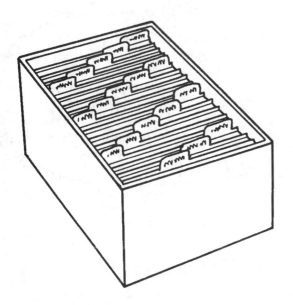 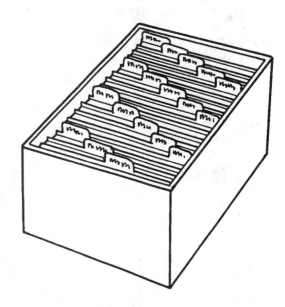

Using Portfolios for Assessment *(cont.)*

If You Moved on to the Showcase Portfolio

If you have reached the stage of the showcase portfolio, the assessment applications will increase dramatically. Since this portfolio has already been sorted and preselected according to some criteria that you and the student have shared, your introductory statement should reflect those decisions. You will also have the benefit of the reflections written by the student about the selected pieces and/or about general growth and progress. You may have chosen to include peer editing statements. You are in a position to have not only an overview and a general feeling of progress but also a good idea of appropriate grades and the material to back up your decisions. This is a wonderful asset when conferencing about grades with parents.

The showcase portfolio is also a great aid in conferencing with students. It gives an enormous boost to the students' self-esteem. Even the student who has not come very far is farther along than at the beginning of the year and can see the possibility of making even more progress. This is the time to set new goals with the student. These plans can be informal or can take the form of a written contract between teacher and student.

If You Have Gotten as Far as the Teacher/Student Portfolio

Here, you are in complete control of your assessment options. You have all the material that is in the student's portfolio plus an assortment of anecdotal records, conference records, interest inventories, test scores of all kinds, and notes of future plans in the form of contracts. A simple process of sorting will give you an overview of both product and process and an excellent background for the grades you will probably need to assign.

The contents of this portfolio can be shared with parents and administrators as well as with the student whose work it represents. Its use encompasses the benefits of the other portfolios and adds a dimension that the others lack—the teacher's considered, professional judgment backed up with evidence.

If You Kept a Teacher Resource Portfolio

Your portfolio of current articles, in-service notes, and other reference material will provide a foundation for many of your assessment decisions. Even if you thought of it first, it is nice to have the opinion of an expert to back up your ideas.

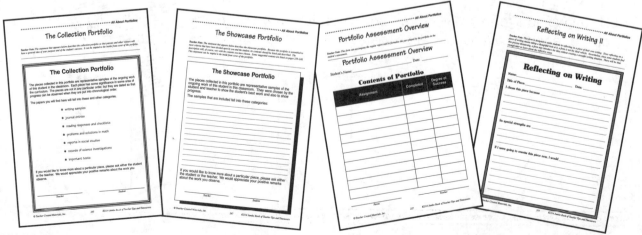

The Collection Portfolio

Teacher Note: The statement that appears below describes the collection portfolio so that parents and other visitors will have a general idea of your purpose and of the student's success. It can be stapled to the inside front cover of the portfolio.

The Collection Portfolio

The pieces collected in this portfolio are representative samples of the ongoing work of this student in the classroom. Each piece has some significance in some area of the curriculum. The pieces are not in any particular order, but they are dated so that progress can be observed when they are put into chronological order.

The papers you will find here will fall into these and other categories.

* writing samples

* journal entries

* reading responses and checklists

* problems and solutions in math

* reports in social studies

* records of science investigations

* important tests

If you would like to know more about a particular piece, please ask either the student or the teacher. We would appreciate your positive remarks about the work you observe.

_____
Teacher

_____
Student

The Writing Process

Teacher Note: *The statement that appears below includes a description of the writing process. It will clarify the inclusion in a portfolio of pieces in various stages of completion. It can be stapled to the inside front cover of a portfolio devoted to language arts or placed at the front of the writing section of a more general portfolio.*

The Writing Process

The pieces of writing in this portfolio reflect the different stages in the writing process. Some are quick-writes, some are edited and revised drafts, and some are completed and polished pieces that have been through the entire writing process.

→ exposure to background information

→ brainstorming

→ first draft

→ peer editing

→ self-editing

→ revision

→ rewriting

→ completion

We hope you will be as interested in the process as in the pieces that are obviously finished.

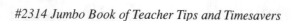

Teacher	*Student*

The Showcase Portfolio

Teacher Note: The statement that appears below describes the showcase portfolio. Because this portfolio is assembled to meet criteria that have been decided upon by you and the student, its contents should be listed and described. The description will, of course, vary with the contents you have chosen. Some suggested contents are listed on pages 239–240. This statement can be stapled to the inside front cover of the portfolio.

The Showcase Portfolio

The pieces collected in this portfolio are representative samples of the ongoing work of this student in this classroom. They were chosen by the student and teacher to show the student's best work and also to show progress.

The samples that are included fall into these categories:

_____
_____
_____
_____
_____
_____
_____
_____
_____
_____
_____
_____
_____

If you would like to know more about a particular piece, please ask either the student or the teacher. We would appreciate your positive remarks about the work you observe.

_____   _____
Teacher   Student

Interest Inventory

Teacher Note: This form is designed to help the student and teacher to identify interests that will motivate reading and writing. It can be personalized for a student or class by adding items that seem appropriate.

Interest Inventory

Name: _____ Date: _____

My favorite subject in school is _____

After school, I like to _____

My favorite hobby is _____

My favorite sport to play is _____

My favorite sport to watch is _____

My favorite sports figure is _____

My best friend's name is _____

The animal I like best is _____

My favorite television show is _____

My favorite movie is _____

My favorite book is _____

The food I like best is _____

The most interesting place I ever went was _____

_____

My best vacation was _____

_____

If I could meet a famous person, it would be _____

_____

If I could do anything I wanted to, I would _____

_____

Contract

Teacher Note: This form is designed to introduce the primary student to the idea of the contract. Agreement can be reached orally and specific assignments written in by the teacher during a conference with the student.

Contract

I have just finished _____

_____.

The next thing I will do in _____

is _____

_____.

I will have this done by my next conference on

_____.

_____
Student

_____
Date

School Contract

Contract

Teacher Note: This form is designed to help the teacher use student conferencing time to its best advantage by having the student make a definite commitment to his or her next steps in the learning process. This contract is intended for the middle and upper elementary grades.

Contract

Having just completed_____

_____,

my next steps in the area of _____

are _____

_____

_____.

I agree to complete these assignments by_____,

which is the date of my next conference.

_____
            Student

_____
            Date

Learning Contract

Evaluation of the Teacher

Teacher Note: This form is designed to assist students in responding to a request for an evaluation of their teacher. This process can be a real help to authentic assessment and can be approached by asking students to do a quick-write. However, the first few times around, it is often helpful to guide the responses a little by offering the students a form.

Evaluation of the Teacher

Teacher's Name: _____ Date: _____

	Never	Sometimes	Usually	Mostly	Always
Is fair	1	2	3	4	5
Is patient	1	2	3	4	5
Explains things well	1	2	3	4	5
Takes time with me	1	2	3	4	5
Listens	1	2	3	4	5
Cares about kids	1	2	3	4	5
Is kind	1	2	3	4	5
Is interesting	1	2	3	4	5
Is organized	1	2	3	4	5
Is pleasant	1	2	3	4	5

Reflecting on Writing I

Teacher Note: This form is designed to introduce the idea of reflecting on a piece of one's own writing to the primary student. The ideas may be shared orally with the teacher who can fill in the information.

Reflecting on Writing

Name: _____ Date: _____

Title of Piece: _____

I want this piece in my portfolio because _____

_____

_____

_____

_____ .

My favorite sentence or part is _____

_____

_____

_____

_____

_____

_____ .

Reflecting on Writing II

Teacher Note: This form is designed to assist students in reflecting on a piece of their own writing. Since reflecting on a piece of writing means taking a thoughtful look at it, a form is not the ideal vehicle. Nevertheless, since some students find this process threatening, a form may introduce the idea without creating a stressful writing situation. There will be time enough later to learn about the reflective essay.

Reflecting on Writing

Name:_____ Date: _____

Title of Piece:_____

I chose this piece because _____

_____

_____

_____

_____.

Its special strengths are _____

_____

_____

_____.

If I were going to rewrite this piece now, I would _____

_____

_____

_____

_____

_____.

Reflecting on Progress in Writing

Teacher Note: This form is designed to assist students in reflecting on their general progress in writing. Since reflection tends to be a subjective process, a form is not the ideal vehicle for reflecting on general progress any more than it is ideal for reflecting on a particular piece. However, the form may help to introduce the idea in this area also.

Reflecting on Progress in Writing

Name: _____ Date: _____

During _____, my writing improved in

(circle one or more)

fluency **organization** **creativity** **clarity** **mechanics**

This improvement can be noticed because_____

_____

_____

_____

_____.

During the next _____,

I plan to work on_____

_____

_____

_____

_____

_____.

Introductory Letter to Parents

*Teacher Note: Write your own letter or use this one to introduce parents to portfolios and portfolio assessment. Send the letter home during the first week of school. **Note:** Be sure to have your principal sign the letter as well if that is the policy in your school.*

Dear Parents,

Welcome to the new school year. We are planning many exciting activities for your child and for you, too.

I am about to introduce portfolios and portfolio evaluation to the students in my classroom. When we were students, it is likely that our work was kept in some sort of folder or file in the classroom. Today portfolios go a step further. They have become widely recognized tools for helping students achieve their best work.

Portfolio evaluation will be explained at Back-to-School Night. However, if you would like to know more about it before then, please feel free to stop by the classroom to see the beginning stages in action.

I look forward to having your child in my class this year. With your interest and cooperation, I know it will be a wonderful year for all of us.

Sincerely yours,

_____

"Kid-Watcher" Form

Teacher Note: "Kid-watching" is a term commonly used when keeping anecdotal records of students. Hand this form to visiting administrators, teachers, and parents so that their observations can be added to your own. You, of course, will decide the weight to place on these observations.

"Kid-Watcher" Form

"Kid-watching" or observing students in the act of learning is an official part of our assessment. Please observe the activities going on in the room and make notes on this form. You may concentrate on your own child or on the whole group. Please place this form on my desk before you leave. Many thanks!

Sincerely,

_____

Learning activity/subject I observed:

_____

Name of student or type of group (large, small, cooperative, partners, etc.):

_____

Please describe what the student(s) was doing.

_____

_____

What was most interesting to you about this observation?

_____

_____

_____

_____   _____
Official Kid-Watcher   *Date of Observation*

Portfolio Assessment Overview

Teacher Note: This form can accompany the regular report card to formalize the part played by the portfolio in the student's assessment.

Portfolio Assessment Overview

Student's Name: _____ Date: _____

Contents of Portfolio

Assignment	Completed	Degree of Success

_____   _____
Parent   *Teacher*

Portfolio Viewing Parent Letter

Date:_____

Dear Parent,

Your child has brought home his or her portfolio for your review. Please look through its contents together with your child. Ask questions of your child as you go so that you understand the contents and the reasons for their inclusion. Afterwards, please respond to the portfolio on the next form. I am eager to read your reaction to the progress your child has made.

Because the portfolio is part of our ongoing instructional program, please return it the next day.

Thank you for your help and cooperation. Remember, I am always available to answer any questions.

Sincerely yours,

_____

Parent Response Form I

Teacher Note: This form can become part of your records after the parent has reviewed the portfolio at home. It will provide a good indication of how well you have been communicating about portfolio assessment.

Parent Response Form

Date:_____

Name of Student: _____

Please answer the following questions.

- Did your child review the portfolio with you? _____

- What part of the portfolio did you like best? _____

  _____

- Did your child's progress come as a surprise to you? Why?

  _____

  _____

- Do you have questions about anything in the portfolio?

  _____

  _____

  _____

I have reviewed the portfolio and am returning it with this form.

  _____
  Parent

Parent Response Form II

Teacher Note: This form can become part of your records after the parent has reviewed the portfolio with you at school. You can ask the questions of the parent while conferencing, jotting down the answers, or you can give the parent a few minutes afterwards to write the responses. It will provide a good indication of how effective portfolios are in communicating student progress to a parent.

Parent Response Form

Date:_____

Name of Student: _____

Please answer the following questions.

✧ Have you previously discussed portfolios with your child?

_____

_____

✧ What part of the portfolio did you like best?

_____

_____

✧ Did your child's progress come as a surprise to you? Why?

_____

_____

✧ Do you have any remaining questions about anything in the portfolio?

_____

_____

✧ Do you fully understand the function of the portfolio in our classroom?

_____

_____

_____
Parent

End-of-Year Letter on Showcase Portfolios

This letter can be sent home with a showcase portfolio at the end of the year.

Dear Parents,

Thank you for your support and interest in our portfolio program. Your efforts contributed toward making it a success. Your child, of course, is the one who has benefited most from this success.

Please encourage your child to keep reading and writing over vacation. Practice in reading and writing is always helpful in maintaining the progress achieved in building new skills. Encourage the continuation of a portfolio in any form you like. Keeping records of our best work, in whatever capacity, can be gratifying as well as inspiring us to continue our achievements.

I hope that you will want to save this portfolio. It will provide a foundation for next year. You and your child can look back on this work and marvel at all the progress.

Thank you for sharing your child with me.

Sincerely yours,

_____

Portfolio Party Invitation

Teacher Note: If interest starts to fade or the students need a lift, consider hosting a Portfolio Party. Parents are invited, of course, but you might also consider inviting the principal or another class. You can serve punch and cookies and make it a real occasion!

You are cordially invited to our Portfolio Party.

Where: _____

_____

When: _____

_____

Our portfolios will be on display, and refreshments will be served.

Recordkeeping

Recordkeeping is an essential part of assessment. However, today's recordkeeping is different from what has been done traditionally. It must be responsive to what the students are doing. The classroom teacher, acting as a facilitator, provides time for completing tasks, helps students to refocus, and provides a sense of criteria by conferencing with students. The records that are kept must represent the range of achievement, the processes that are going on, the effort that is shown, and the improvement that is demonstrated. Most of this recordkeeping is done simply by selecting appropriate samples for the student's portfolio, but these samples are even more meaningful when they are supported by checklists, conferencing notes, and anecdotal records.

Positive Recordkeeping

In the past, anecdotal records were most commonly used to document behavior problems. Today the primary use of anecdotal records is positive. The comments are designed to describe progress and achievements, giving a personal flavor to assessment records.

Part of the Instructional Day

Ongoing assessment and recordkeeping must be built into the school day. They take part of what is commonly thought of as "instructional time" because they are, in fact, part of instruction and not a separate activity. Having forms at hand and using them as you go will make this kind of assessment work for you.

Using Forms

Sample recordkeeping forms are included on the following pages. Pages 264–279 are for teacher use and pages 280–292 are for student use. The wording on the forms is designed to trigger your thought processes as well as those of your students. You may, however, prefer to personalize the forms with your own wording or use totally blank forms. Once you start, you will find what is most comfortable and effective for you.

In each case, a sample or two is filled out to show the type of responses you might want to record. These samples follow the blank forms for you to duplicate and use.

Dating Records

Most important of all, date every piece of paper you write on whether it is a form or a blank page. You cannot hope to demonstrate progress if you do not know which observation was made first, last, or in between. The importance of dating cannot be stressed too strongly.

Some Words to the Wise

Resist the temptation to keep anecdotal records, conference notes, or anything else that might be important someday on scraps or even half sheets of paper. Nothing will compensate for losing a vital piece of paper in the paper avalanche that may threaten to overwhelm any teacher just beginning to keep anecdotal records.

Consider color-coding. Run forms for anecdotal records on one color, forms for recording the results of conferencing on another, student forms such as checklists and reflections on still another, and so forth. With this method your sorting is almost done for you.

Anecdotal Record Form

Teacher Note: *This form can be duplicated and used for anecdotal recordkeeping. Samples of its use are modeled on the next two pages.*

Anecdotal Record Form

Date:_____

Student's Name:_____

Subject:_____

Instructional Situation: _____

Instructional Task: _____

Behavior Observed:_____

_____

_____

_____

_____

_____

This behavior was important because _____

_____

_____

_____

_____

_____

Anecdotal Record Form *(cont.)*

Teacher Note: *This is a sample of how the previous anecdotal record form can be used in a classroom situation.*

Anecdotal Record Form

Date: *1/9*

Student's Name: *Becky Johnson*

Subject: *math*

Instructional Situation: *large group*

Instructional Task: *one-on-one correspondence*

Behavior Observed: *Becky counted five blocks, touching each one as she counted. I took the blocks and gave her back two. She said, "I need three more to make five."*

This behavior was important because *this is a breakthrough into number sense for Becky.*

Anecdotal Record Form (cont.)

Teacher Note: *This is another sample of how the same form can be used in a different classroom situation.*

Anecdotal Record Form

Date: <u>11/20</u>

Student's Name: <u>Shantell Nolen</u>

Subject: <u>language arts</u>

Instructional Situation: <u>cooperative learning groups</u>

Instructional Task: <u>peer editing</u>

Behavior Observed: <u>Shantell was able to identify errors in punctuation and suggest corrections. She used a positive approach: "Do you think it would help if . . .?"</u>

This behavior was important because <u>it shows growth in both the mechanics of writing and in good social skills. She was really aware of her success!</u>

Student Conference Record for Reading

Teacher Note: This form can be duplicated and used for reading conference recordkeeping. Samples of its use are modeled on the next two pages.

Student Conference Record for Reading

Date: _____

Student's Name: _____

What is the title of the book you are reading?

_____

Who wrote it? _____

Have you read other books by this author? _____

Why did you choose this book? _____

_____

Tell me something about the story so far.

_____

_____

_____

What would you like to do when you finish this book? (Options: write a report, draw a poster, give an oral report to the class, write a letter to the author, etc.)

_____

Would you like to read another book by the same author? Why?

_____

_____

Teacher Comments: _____

_____

_____

_____

Student Conference Record for Reading *(cont.)*

Teacher Note: This is a sample of how the previous record form for student conferences can be used in response to a student's reading.

Student Conference Record for Reading

Date: *2/7*

Student's Name: *Brent Tanner*

What is the title of the book you are reading?
The Wind in the Willows

Who wrote it? *Kenneth Grahame*

Have you read other books by this author? *no*

Why did you choose this book? *My best friend said it was "neat."*

Tell me something about the story so far.
It's about this rat and his friends, Mole and Toad. It's the same toad as "Mr. Toad's Wild Ride." They have adventures.

What would you like to do when you finish this book? (Options: write a report, draw a poster, give an oral report to the class, write a letter to the author, etc.)
an oral report with puppets

Would you like to read another book by the same author? Why?
Yes. It's sort of an older kid's fairy tale.

Teacher Comments: *Brent really raised his reading level for this one. I'm excited for him.*

Student Conference Record for Reading *(cont.)*

Student Conference Record for Reading

Date: _10/28_

Student's Name: _Tyler Armour_

What is the title of the book you are reading?

Farmer Boy

Who wrote it? _Laura Ingalls Wilder_

Have you read other books by this author? _no_

Why did you choose this book? _My mother wanted me to read it._

Tell me something about the story so far.

It's about this boy and his family who live on a farm more than a hundred years ago. It tells all about how they do stuff on the farm. They eat a lot, too! He must work hard to be able to eat all that food!

What would you like to do when you finish this book? (Options: write a report, draw a poster, give an oral report to the class, write a letter to the author, etc.)

I'm going to make a book poster for the library.

Would you like to read another book by the same author? Why?

I'm going to read all of them. They're pretty interesting. It makes me imagine that I'm there.

Teacher Comments: _Tyler reads well and widely. He finishes one author's book before going on to another author's work._

Student Conference Record for Reading

Teacher Note: This form can be duplicated and used for writing conference recordkeeping. Samples of its use are modeled on the next two pages.

Student Conference Record for Writing

Date: _____

Student's Name: _____

What is the title of the piece you are working on now?

_____

What kind of piece is it? (story, poem, essay, report, etc.)

_____

How far have you gotten in the writing process? (pre-writing, rough draft, self-editing, peer editing, revising, ready for publishing)

_____

What do you plan to do next with this piece?

_____

_____

What do you like best about this piece?

_____

_____

Is there anything you would like to change on this piece?

_____

_____

Teacher Comments: _____

_____

_____

_____

Student Conference Record for Reading *(cont.)*

Teacher Note: This is a sample of how the previous record form for student conferences can be used in response to a student's writing.

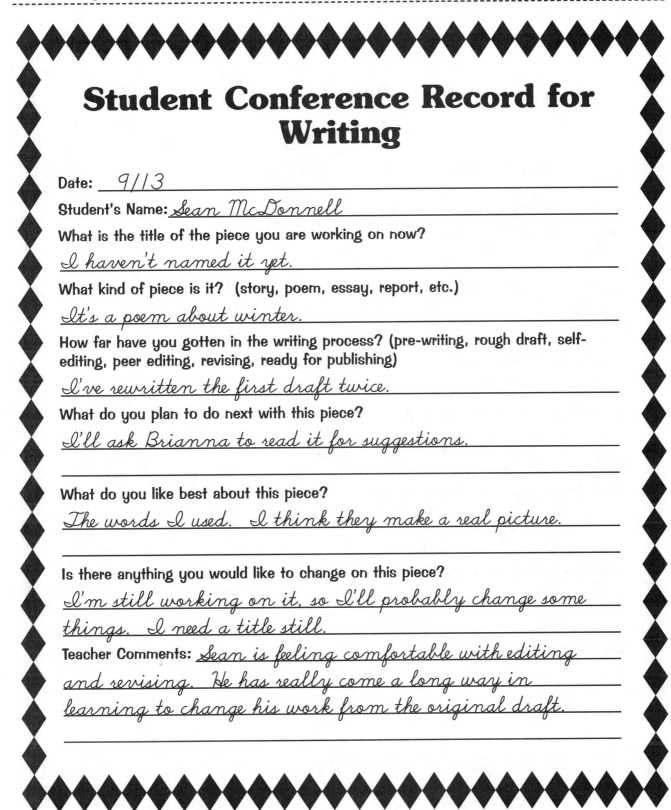

Student Conference Record for Writing

Date: 9/13

Student's Name: Sean McDonnell

What is the title of the piece you are working on now?

I haven't named it yet.

What kind of piece is it? (story, poem, essay, report, etc.)

It's a poem about winter.

How far have you gotten in the writing process? (pre-writing, rough draft, self-editing, peer editing, revising, ready for publishing)

I've rewritten the first draft twice.

What do you plan to do next with this piece?

I'll ask Brianna to read it for suggestions.

What do you like best about this piece?

The words I used. I think they make a real picture.

Is there anything you would like to change on this piece?

I'm still working on it, so I'll probably change some things. I need a title still.

Teacher Comments: Sean is feeling comfortable with editing and revising. He has really come a long way in learning to change his work from the original draft.

Student Conference Record for Reading (cont.)

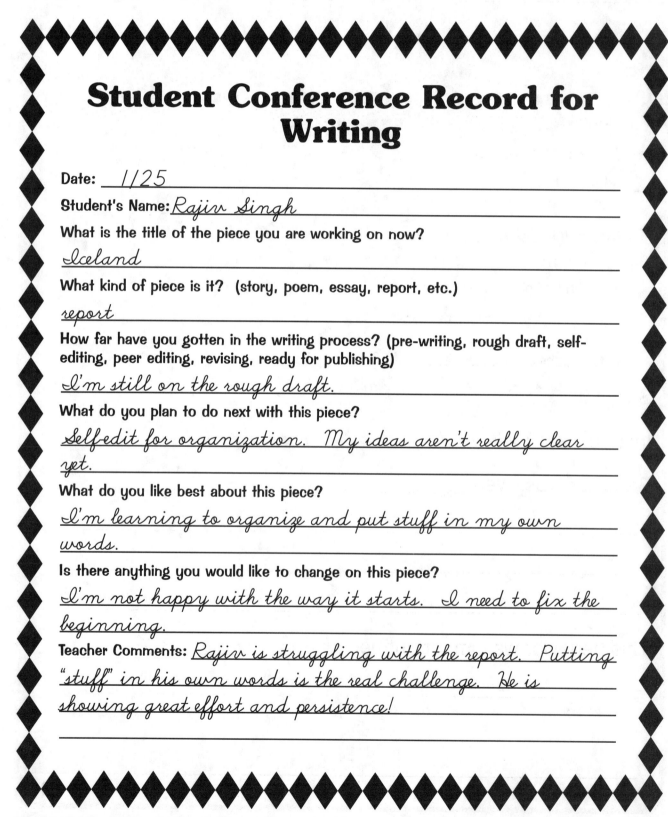

Student Conference Record for Writing

Date: *1/25*

Student's Name: *Rajiv Singh*

What is the title of the piece you are working on now?

Iceland

What kind of piece is it? (story, poem, essay, report, etc.)

report

How far have you gotten in the writing process? (pre-writing, rough draft, self-editing, peer editing, revising, ready for publishing)

I'm still on the rough draft.

What do you plan to do next with this piece?

Self-edit for organization. My ideas aren't really clear yet.

What do you like best about this piece?

I'm learning to organize and put stuff in my own words.

Is there anything you would like to change on this piece?

I'm not happy with the way it starts. I need to fix the beginning.

Teacher Comments: *Rajiv is struggling with the report. Putting "stuff" in his own words is the real challenge. He is showing great effort and persistence!*

Small-Group Record Form

**Teacher Note:** This form can be duplicated and used for records of small-group activities. Samples of its use are modeled on the next two pages.

Small-Group Record Form

Date: _____

Kind of Group (*cooperative learning, partners, etc.*)

_____

Names of Students:

_____   _____

_____   _____

_____   _____

Subject: _____

Instructional Task: _____

Behavior Observed: _____

_____

_____

_____

This behavior was important because _____

_____

_____

_____

Small-Group Record Form (cont.)

Teacher Note: This is a sample of how the previous record form for small-group activities can be used when observing group interaction and learning.

Small-Group Record Form

Date: *3/5*

Kind of Group (*cooperative learning, partners, etc.*)

partners

Names of Students:

Liu Ping   *Doretta Green*

Subject: *language arts*

Instructional Task: *dialogue journals*

Behavior Observed: *The girls took turns reading and writing replies in each other's journals. There was a discussion of the importance of correct spelling.*

This behavior was important because *the girls both agreed that spelling had a function in expressing meaning clearly. Up until now, they had not seen a practical reason for learning or editing spelling.*

Small-Group Record Form (cont.)

Teacher Note: This is a sample of how the previous record form for small-group activities can be used when observing individual learning within a small group.

Small-Group Record Form

Date: _5/6_

Kind of Group (*cooperative learning, partners, etc.*)

cooperative learning

Names of Students:

Connor McNiff   _Steven Chon_

Matthew Wallace

Andrew Buss

Subject: _math_

Instructional Task: _round-robin multiplication tables_

Behavior Observed: _Andrew was able to name each step of the table that came his way. He appeared calm and confident._

This behavior was important because _he has always struggled with the tables, his lack of confidence getting in the way of his concentration. He has obviously been studying, and his confidence is showing._

Large-Group Record Form

Teacher Note: This form can be duplicated and used for records of large-group or whole-class instruction. A sample of its use is modeled on the next page.

Large-Group Record Form

Date: _____

Assignment: _____

Instructional Goal: _____

Class List	Completed	Degree of Success	Action to Be Taken

Large-Group Record Form (cont.)

Teacher Note: This is a sample of how the previous record form for large-group observation can be used.

Large-Group Record Form

Date: 11/30

Assignment: Open-Ended Reading Test-Unit 1

Instructional Goal: to assess comprehension

Class List	Completed	Degree of Success	Action to Be Taken
Alvane, Lupe	✓	good	go on
Beghon, Hamden	✓	fair	small-group review*
Ferber, Flora	near	—	work with aide-test
Gozzi, Bill	✓	fair	small-group review*
Kajima, Ben	✓	good	go on
Levy, Sara	✓	excellent	conference to set new goals
McRae, Lisa	✓	good	go on
Ngo, Lang	✓	fair	small-group review*
Parker, Michael	✓	fair	small-group review*
Santos, Justino	✓	excellent	conference to set new goals
Trapp, Jerry	✓	good	go on
Whittingham, Ann	no	—	conference to determine problem
*Call group on Tuesday morning.			

Cooperative Groups Rating Sheet

Teacher Note: This is an example of a chart that can be used to rate cooperative learning groups in a variety of settings. On this form, the groups are numbered. A model of this completed form is included on the next page.

Cooperative Groups Rating Sheet

Date: _____   Activity: _____

Cooperative Group Characteristics	Group								
	1	2	3	4	5	6	7	8	9
Works in a timely way									
Everyone participates									
Knows job									
Solves own group problems									
Everyone cooperates									
Keeps noise level down									
Encouragement seen/heard									

Teacher comments: _____

_____

_____

_____

Cooperative Groups Rating Sheet *(cont.)*

Teacher Note: This is a sample of how the previous form for rating cooperative groups can be used.

Cooperative Groups Rating Sheet

Date: *1/14*   Activity: *writing original fables*

Cooperative Group Characteristics	Group								
	1	2	3	4	5	6	7	8	9
Works in a timely way	x	x	x	x		x	x	x	x
Everyone participates		x	x	x	x	x		x	x
Knows job	x		x	x		x	x		x
Solves own group problems	x		x		x	x	x	x	x
Everyone cooperates	x	x	x	x	x	x	x	x	x
Keeps noise level down	x	x				x		x	
Encouragement seen/heard		x		x					x

Teacher comments: *Aside from minor problem-solving difficulty, all groups really worked together well, doing excellent work. Their final products are thorough and well done.*

Reading Response I

Teacher Note: This reading response form is designed for the child in primary grades. It can be filled out by the teacher during a conference for the K–1 student or by the student once he or she has achieved a certain level of writing mastery. Some older primary students may prefer to use the version designed for upper grades. A completed model of this form can be found on the next page.

Reading Response

Name: _____

Date: _____

I read _____

by _____.

It has_____pages.

It is   easy   just right   hard   to read.

I want to   ___ do something
                                   different:_____

___ make an oral report.

___ make a written   _____
       report.   _____

___ draw a picture of my   _____
       favorite part.
                                       _____

The next book I want to read is_____

_____.

Reading Response I *(cont.)*

Teacher Note: This is a sample of how the previous reading response form can be used.

Reading Response

Name: <u>Judy Rosen</u>

Date: <u>Dec. 10</u>

I read <u>Danny and the Dinosaur</u>

by <u>Syd Hoff.</u>

It has <u>   64   </u> pages.

It is   easy   (just right)   hard   to read.

I want to   ___ do something different:_____

  ___ make an oral report.

  ___ make a written report.   _____

  <u>X</u> draw a picture of my favorite part.   _____

             _____

The next book I want to read is <u>Mike Mulligan and</u>

<u>His Steam Shovel by Virginia Lee Burton.</u>

Reading Response II

Teacher Note: This reading response form is designed for the child in the middle and upper elementary grades and can be filled out by the student. A completed model of this form can be found on the next page.

Reading Response

Name: _____

Date: _____

Title: _____

Author: _____

Number of Pages: _____

Did you enjoy this book? Explain. _____

_____

_____

Tell about your favorite part of the book. _____

_____

_____

Will you read more books by this author? _____

_____

How will you report on the book? (*book report, library poster, diorama, oral report, etc.*) _____

_____

Reading Response II *(cont.)*

Teacher Note: This is a sample of how the previous reading response form can be used.

Reading Response

Name: Kenny Walsh

Date: February 27

Title: James and the Giant Peach

Author: Roald Dahl

Number of Pages: 126

Did you enjoy this book? Explain. I enjoyed this book because it is full of adventure, and it is interesting.

Tell about your favorite part of the book. My favorite part is when James and his bug friends go out to sea after the peach rolls down the hill. This part is fun to imagine. They are in the sea, and a shark is trying to rip the peach and eat them. They think of a good idea to save themselves when some seagulls fly by.

Will you read more books by this author? Yes, I have read more Roald Dahl books, and I will read more in the future.

How will you report on the book? *(book report, library poster, diorama, oral report, etc.)* I will make a library poster. I will include James and his friends standing on the peach and having fun.

Student Reading Record I

Teacher Note: *This form can be duplicated and used for primary students to keep records of their reading. Teachers or adult aides may write while pre- and beginning writers dictate, or students with enough writing mastery may keep their own records.*

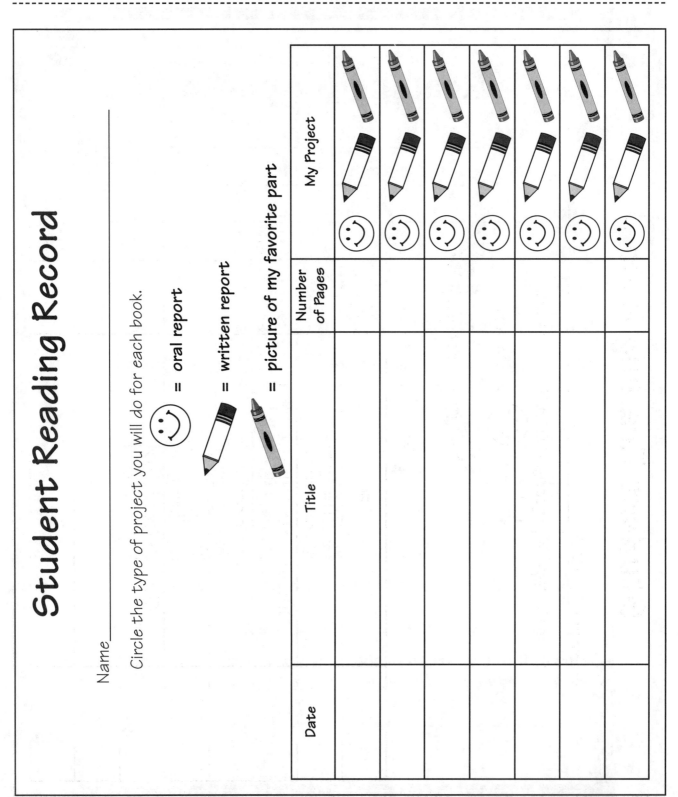

Student Reading Record 1 *(cont.)*

Teacher Note: This is a sample of how the previous reading record can be used by primary students to record their reading and their proposals for reading reports.

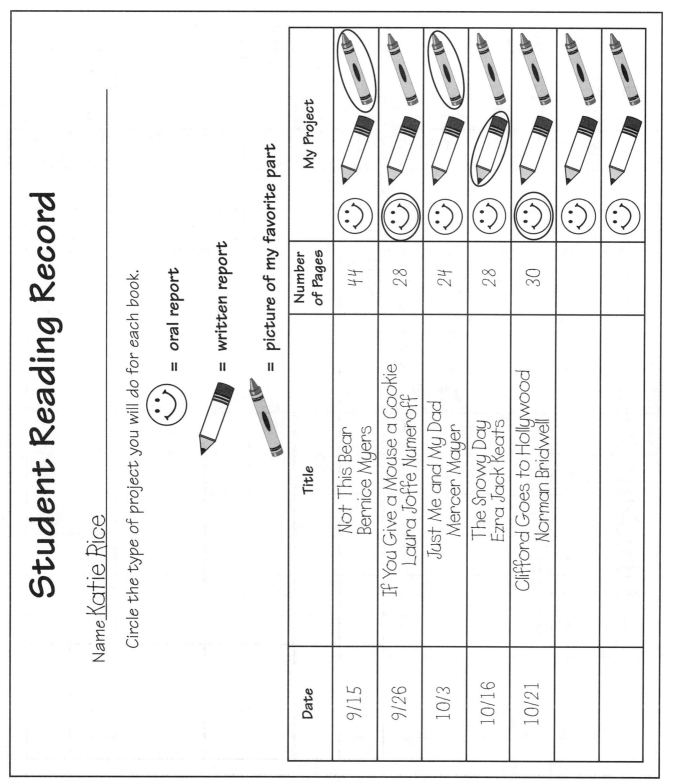

Student Reading Record

Name Katie Rice

Circle the type of project you will do for each book.

☺ = oral report

✏ = written report

🖍 = picture of my favorite part

Date	Title	Number of Pages	My Project		
9/15	Not This Bear Bernice Myers	44	☺	✏	(🖍)
9/26	If You Give a Mouse a Cookie Laura Joffe Numeroff	28	(☺)	✏	🖍
10/3	Just Me and My Dad Mercer Mayer	24	☺	✏	🖍
10/16	The Snowy Day Ezra Jack Keats	28	(☺)	(✏)	🖍
10/21	Clifford Goes to Hollywood Norman Bridwell	30	☺	✏	🖍

Student Reading Record II

Teacher Note: This form can be duplicated and used for middle and upper elementary students to keep records of their reading.

- -

Student Reading Record

Name: _____

Date	Title	# of Pages	Proposed Response to Book (*written/oral report or other*)

Student Reading Record II *(cont.)*

Teacher Note: This is a sample of how the previous reading record can be used by students to record their reading and their proposals for reading reports.

- -

Student Reading Record

Name: Jeff Lyons

Date	Title	# of Pages	Proposed Response to Book (*written/oral report or other*)
9/10	Stuart Little	131	written report
9/30	Charlotte's Web	184	oral report
10/21	East o' the Sun	288	(didn't finish book)
11/15	The Wizard of Oz	209	poster for library
12/10	The Mad Scientists' Club	186	

Writing Checklist I

Teacher Note: This writing checklist is for student use in the primary grades. It can be stapled on the inside back cover of the student's portfolio and filled out during a conference for pre- and beginning writers. Students with enough writing competency can make their own notations. Older students may prefer to use the checklist for the higher grades.

Writing Checklist

Name: _____ Grade _____

Date	Writing Assignment	Editing	Revising	Comments

Writing Checklist I *(cont.)*

Teacher Note: This is a sample of how the previous writing checklist can be used to record a student's progress through the writing process.

Writing Checklist

Name: Marta Ramirez   Grade   3

Date	Writing Assignment	Editing	Revising	Comments
9/10	autobiographical incident: "Summer"	9/11	9/14	Good job!
9/17	quick-write: "Fall"	—	—	Nice
9/25	story: "The Bike Ride"	9/27	9/30	Interesting story
10/10	essay: "Why I Like School"	10/15	10/16	☺
10/20	poem: "Halloween"	—	10/26	Great!
11/10	report: "Pilgrims"	11/12	11/15	Used three sources

Writing Checklist II

Teacher Note: This writing checklist is for student use in the middle and upper elementary grades. It can be stapled on the inside back cover of the student's folder or notebook.

Writing Checklist

Name: _____

Date Begun	Writing Assignment	First Draft	Peer Edit	Revision	Self-Edit	Revision	Last Draft	Comments

Writing Checklist II *(cont.)*

Teacher Note: This writing checklist is for student use in the middle and upper elementary grades. It can be stapled on the inside back cover of the student's folder or notebook.

Writing Checklist

Name: Cassie Jackson

Date Begun	Writing Assignment	First Draft	Peer Edit	Revision	Self-Edit	Revision	Last Draft	Comments
9/10	observational- "My Favorite Place"	9/11	9/16	9/17	9/23	9/25	—	I used good words to describe.
9/13	quick-write- "What I Want to Learn This Year"	—	—	—	—	—	—	—
9/18	poem- "Fall Colors"	9/18	—	—	9/19	9/20	9/20	This was fun!

Rubrics

Here is a sample of a holistic rubric you can use when marking student writing in any area of the curriculum. Give each student a copy of the rubric so students know what the number grade equates to.

Writing Rubric

6—This writing is creative, detailed, and complete. The spelling, punctuation, and form are correct.

5—This writing is complete. The spelling, punctuation, and form are correct.

4—This writing is adequate. There is a good use of correct spelling, punctuation, and form with just one or two areas that need improvement.

3—This writing is not complete. It has potential, but more information and editing are needed.

2—This writing has little to do with the topic. It is disorganized and needs correcting.

1—This writing is off the topic and needs a great deal of work.

Reading Aloud

Reading aloud is the single most important activity for building the knowledge for eventual reading success. Reading aloud makes reading a pleasurable experience instead of a chore. As adults read aloud, children see positive reading role models, gain new information, are exposed to books, and experience the emotions elicited by the literature. Reading aloud to children must be part of every elementary teacher's daily program. The frequency and length of read-aloud sessions will vary according to the maturity level of your students. Be aware that every minute of this time is valuable as it stimulates imagination, stretches attention span, improves listening comprehension, nurtures emotional development, and establishes the very important reading-writing connection.

When reading aloud to your class, remember to do the following:

- Use words like "title," "title page," "publisher," etc., when introducing books.

- Read the same books over and over again.

- Include old favorites as well as a new book every day. Occasionally read books with a richer vocabulary and a more complex story line than most of your other read-aloud books.

- Include fairy tales in your collection of read-aloud books. Read several different versions of the same fairy tale.

- Invite a more able student or another adult to read aloud.

- Have a world map near your read-aloud area. Point out where particular stories originate or are set.

- With some selections discuss setting, characters, main idea, plot, etc.

- Don't underestimate the children's attention spans.

- Read many kinds of writing, including poetry, newspapers, and magazines.

- Read slowly enough for the child to build a mental picture.

- Bring authors to life by learning and sharing some personal information about them.

- Add an interesting dimension to read-aloud time whenever possible by bringing in something authentic pertaining to the story.

- Read just for the enjoyment of experiencing a good piece of literature.

Silent and Partner Reading

Sustained Silent Reading

Sustained Silent Reading (S.S.R.) is an activity that should be expected every day of all individuals in the classroom. Everyone chooses a book and stays engaged in reading it for a sustained length of time. It is important for students to realize that they are capable of this and that reading can be a form of recreation. This also gives students an opportunity to practice individually what they have been taught.

To facilitate Sustained Silent Reading, the teacher should explain and model the following rules:

❏ Each individual selects one book. (Make available all kinds of books; no trading of books during reading is allowed.)

❏ Each individual reads alone silently. (Realize that younger students tend to subvocalize as they read.)

❏ Adults in the classroom also choose a book and read uninterrupted.

❏ Set a timer to signal the end of S.S.R. Start at five minutes and gradually increase to 15 minutes or more, depending on the maturity of your class.

Partner Reading

Another effective and fun form of reading practice is partner reading. This is a time when students pair up with a classmate or a cross-age buddy to read books of their choice together.

Allow more time for partner reading than for silent reading since time for socialization is necessary. This is a wonderful time for friendships to be established. Encourage positive reinforcement and taking turns.

Some strategies for this include the following:

❏ Study and discuss the illustrations, then together choose the illustration that is the best, scariest, silliest, etc.

❏ Together find the longest word, 10 compound words, other words that mean big, etc.

❏ Read the book, taking turns by sentences or pages.

❏ After sharing the book, ask each other one comprehension question.

❏ Choose a character and tell your partner why you'd like to be that character.

❏ Tell your partner why you like or do not like the book.

Library or Reading Center

A reading center or library is imperative for your classroom. It should be cozy and completely accessible to students. A set of shelves or several receptacles filled with all kinds of books is the main ingredient. You can collect books from book clubs, school and public libraries, and thrift stores or yard sales. Do not forget to include student-authored books as well as the books you have used in previous lessons. Be sure to make available books of various reading levels, from picture books and wordless books to more difficult ones.

I agree to take good care of the books I check out from our classroom library. I will return the books in good condition so that others may read them.

_____
Student signature

A cleanable beanbag chair and pillows with washable cases are wonderful for making children feel at home in the library. Add a stuffed bear so that students always have an "ear" in which to read.

To make an "official" library in your room, purchase some library pockets for the books. (You can find them at teacher supply or stationery stores.) Duplicate the library card on this page and distribute it to the classroom borrowers.

Making the Most of Literature

These steps can be followed when using a piece of literature with children.

Get into the Literature: Provide background experiences and activate students' prior knowledge. To do this you might choose one of the following activities:

- Arouse interest in the story by reading aloud related literature selections that will add to students' conceptual background.
- Relate the topic to personal experiences.
- Provide a hands-on concrete experience like a field trip, a demonstration, or observation of actual artifacts.
- Brainstorm what is already known about a topic to enable students to learn from each other's knowledge and experiences.
- Show a related video, film, or filmstrip dealing with the topic.
- Conduct a related science experiment.
- Role-play social situations that might incite certain feelings which will make the topic or subject more relevant and familiar.

Go Through the Literature: Work with a piece of literature by focusing on meaning and language. In order to accomplish this do the following:

- Share the pictures only. Tell any information you get from the illustrations; make predictions about story content.
- Guide the reading of the selection. Students read a section and then the teacher reads it with the students and discusses it.
- Teach the vocabulary within the context as the class reads the selection.
- Read the selection through echo reading. The teacher reads a line, then students echo (read) the same line.
- Read the selection together and identify parts of the story—characters, setting, plot, etc.
- Read the selection together and discuss it from different characters' points of view.
- Build and rebuild all or part of the story in the pocket chart.
- Read the selection and make up comprehension questions to answer in cooperative groups.

Go Beyond the Literature: Extend and build students' knowledge through discovery and practice. Some activities to accomplish this include the following:

- After reading the selection and working with the print, relate the literature and issues to the students in some way. These "beyond" activities should build on what the students know and cause them to stretch their thoughts and experiences.
- Rewrite the story, making some change in a story part.
- Write in your journal a response about the selection.

- Role-play being a specific character.
- Do a book review on the selection.
- Create an art project related to the selection.
- Make up a song.
- Find a related recipe and cook it.
- Make a big book.
- Dramatize the selection.

Print-Rich Environment

The environment of a classroom should be highly literate and stimulating.

Functional, meaningful, and relevant print is everywhere. Numerous displays throughout the classroom invite the students to read, share, and enjoy. The print found throughout the classroom is "kid friendly." The amount and complexity of print grows with the students, and much of it is created by them. Children learn to read by reading and to write by writing, so it is the teacher's job to provide as many opportunities as possible for reading and writing.

Listed below are suggestions for incorporating the language arts throughout the classroom and making the environment rich in printed materials.

- ❖ Use labels throughout the room to identify objects and serve as references for spelling.

- ❖ Provide at least 100 books for a class of 30 children.

- ❖ Let the children see that you write, to yourself and others, notes that serve specific purposes.

- ❖ Display pertinent information for the students to read (lunch menus, reminders, responsibilities for various members of the class, etc.).

- ❖ Display a message board so that notes to the class can be written. For example, "Don't forget your library book Tuesday."

- ❖ Provide a mailbox to encourage children to write notes to the teacher.

- ❖ Post daily news that the class dictates and publishes.

- ❖ Display books, poems, sentence strips, and songs that have been studied.

- ❖ Prominently display students' written work.

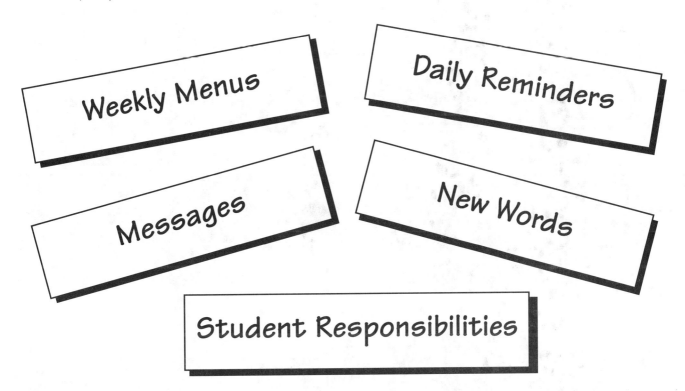

Printed Alphabet

Reproduce a copy for each student to use for reference.

Aa Bb Cc Dd

Ee Ff Gg Hh

Ii Jj Kk Ll

Mm Nn Oo Pp

Qq Rr Ss Tt

Uu Vv Ww Xx

Yy Zz

Cursive Alphabet

Reproduce a copy for each student to use for reference.

Aa Bb Cc Dd

Ee Ff Gg Hh

Ii Jj Kk Ll

Mm Nn Oo Pp

Qq Rr Ss Tt

Uu Vv Ww Xx

Yy Zz

Word Banks

Word banks are collections of related words. They can be displayed in the classroom. Creating and manipulating a word bank provides an excellent opportunity for integrating reading, writing, listening, and speaking. Word banks are created by brainstorming with groups of children. Children build on each other's ideas as they link their prior knowledge with new learning. Brainstorming to create word banks is a meaningful and profitable activity.

As the class brainstorms words children already know about a topic, the words are recorded by the teacher on the chalkboard, chart paper, butcher paper, or individual word cards. The words should be printed large enough to easily be read by students and should be hung in a place that is easily seen. As ideas are recorded, model and discuss skills and strategies for decoding the word. State each word as it is written so that students can see the connections among speech, print, and spelling/phonics. Tie together the speaking, listening, reading, and writing by stating, "I heard you say_____. This is how it is written, and then we can read it." Write the word, say it slowly, and call attention to any phonetic rules that apply.

During this time, large amounts of vocabulary are developed. Each addition to the word bank should be discussed thoroughly. This causes the children to expand or alter their background knowledge and will aid them in manipulating the word bank words. It will also help in using these words accurately in writing and speaking.

Word banks should grow. Whether the collection of words relates to a theme (topic) or is based on a skill (for example, a compound word bank), it should belong to the children. Words should be transferred to individual cards and illustrated by the children so that the cards can be manipulated. They should remain accessible to the children during journal writing or other writing activities.

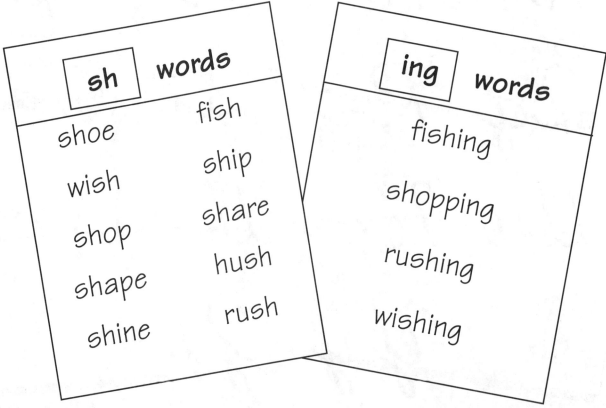

Word Banks *(cont.)*

Manipulation of word banks must occur in a group situation, large or small. This enables students to share ideas, learn from each other, expand or alter the particular schema they have, and develop confidence and needed socialization abilities.

Arranging the word banks into categories makes the words meaningful and causes children to defend their positions and think abstractly. Skills and confidence are gained by such activities. For these types of activities, the words must be on individual word cards. An illustration on each card is extremely helpful. The individual cards can be manipulated in a pocket chart, on the floor or large table area, or on the chalkboard, using reversed masking tape strips. Remember, for the greatest value the word bank should remain available for the students to use in practice and as a reference when writing.

Organizing a group of related words into categories can be done in many ways. Any way is correct as long as the student has an acceptable reason for sorting this way. Categories may include choosing a structural feature of the word (like words with -ing ending), putting the words into alphabetical order, grouping according to conceptual attribute (large animals, small animals) or organizing by largest to smallest word. **Note:** When sorting into categories, be sure to ask "What's the rule for sorting? or "Why do these words go together?" Give ample thinking time.

Nouns

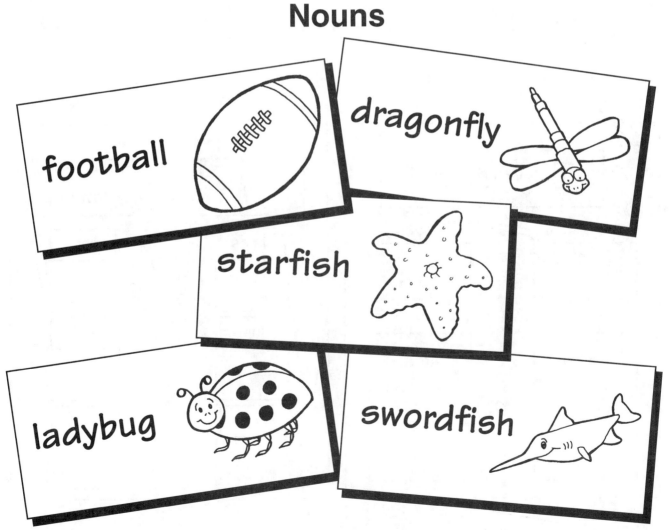

Pocket Charts

Pocket charts are valuable tools for teaching and learning. They may be purchased at teacher-supply stores or ordered from many school product catalogs. They contain clear, plastic pockets through which word cards, picture cards, and/or sentence strips can be seen. Pocket charts make an attractive display for word banks, poems, songs, etc., and help to create a print-rich environment. The words can be used in writing assignments or copied for handwriting practice. Thus, pocket charts are excellent for the integration of the language arts. And, perhaps most importantly, pocket charts provide for easy manipulation of words by students for valuable practice in group or individual situations.

The pocket chart can be utilized very effectively to focus a language arts lesson. The words to a poem, song, or repeated portion of a story can be placed in the chart. Lines of text are clearly separated, enabling students to "track" (follow along with their finger) easily. This aids the child in discovering phonics and the reading-writing connection. Use large, heavy-duty, recloseable, and clear plastic bags to store words and sentences from recent lessons near the pocket chart for students' individual practice. Pocket charts provide for the important shared-reading experience. The use of large printed words in the chart with the students gathered around to read together allows students to see the print and hear the sounds of the language just as in the lap reading done by many parents even before kindergarten. This is important to reading readiness and is difficult for teachers to give to each student individually.

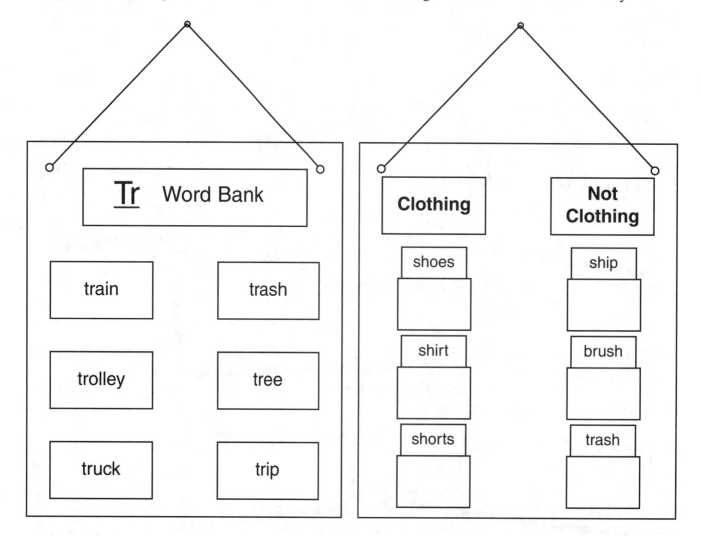

Big Books

Research shows us that a common experience of most good readers is that they were read to as young children. Typically, a child sits on the parent's lap, viewing the pictures and text, while the parent reads. The child's attention is focused on the illustrations and the print as the book is read aloud. Teachers have always read to children, but most children cannot see the text or illustrations clearly during these reading sessions. Big books are a way to involve groups of children so that they form an understanding that the process of reading is print stimulated.

A good shared or "read together" big book should have several of the following:

- ◆ natural spoken language
- ◆ predictable story line
- ◆ rhyme and/or rhythm
- ◆ repetition of phrases

- ◆ illustrations that capture the children's interest
- ◆ print that is big enough to be seen easily by children from a distance of 13' (4 m)

Discovery and Predictions

Discovery includes setting the stage for the first encounter with the story and the illustrations. This can be done by recalling or providing related background experiences. Predictions about the book set up a framework that is confirmed or changed as the story is read. Children learn to become active readers, which is a key to successful reading.

Exploration and Conventions

By exploring and studying the conventions of the printed big book page, children learn the skills required for reading and writing. This includes phonics, punctuation, vocabulary, or any other conventions of writing. To help children master the basic process of reading, the teacher can use such techniques as the following:

- ◆ Encourage responses and ask questions about the story.

- ◆ Point to each word as the book is reread. (This step is crucial in the early grades.)

- ◆ Ask questions about the format of the printed word, such as "Where do we begin on a page?" "Which way do we go?" or "Why are there blank spaces between words?"

- ◆ Pause before a predictable word and allow the children to fill it in.

Extensions

Rewrite and re-illustrate the story with the children, act it out, and/or discuss the sequence of the story. Make or purchase matching little books to use with individuals or small groups. Use the story as a theme for a unit. This unit can extend across the curriculum to cover math, science, art, music, poetry, movement, cooking activities, etc.

Independence

Place big books and accompanying little books (commercial, teacher- or child-produced) in the classroom for all children to experiment with and use for independent reading or recreational browsing. Record the stories and place the tapes and books at a listening center. Provide an opportunity for children to check out the books and take them home overnight.

Dictionary on the Wall

The main purpose of Dictionary on the Wall is for students to have easy access to correct spelling of frequently used but difficult-to-spell words. Alphabetizing is an important skill taught through this activity. Students also gain confidence in finding needed information independently and experience repeated practice at correctly writing words that must be memorized.

In order to display a Dictionary on the Wall, a large alphabet (like the traditional alphabet letters displayed above the chalkboard in many classrooms) is needed. A 12" (30 cm) space below or above each letter is necessary for posting words. The location of the alphabet and accompanying Dictionary on the Wall should be central so that children can see to copy the words while writing. Words posted should be those used frequently by the students in their writing.

As students repeatedly copy these words from the wall, they will become less and less dependent on looking up at them. Soon most students will have internalized the correct spellings of the words. Once you notice that most of the students have mastered the spelling of a word, take it down to make room for another needed word.

had has	if in is	jar job	kite
Hh	**Ii**	**Jj**	**Kk**

Sample Word List

the	would	an	have	in	into	do	one
you	look	if	but	was	go	about	all
are	no	then	your	they	my	some	there
a	of	make	which	from	is	time	how
had	that	two	up	not	for	see	our
were	as	way	these	can	I	than	her
use	be	to	him	she	or	over	has
their	by	he	write	other	what	on	number
many	we	his	people	so	said	part	first

Spelling and Phonics

Understanding the phonics of our language system is crucial to both reading and writing. In working toward the goal of helping students to become more successful writers and readers, spelling and phonics must be addressed. Writing is the natural way to explore the phonics of language. Frequent writing will do more to increase spelling achievement than any other single activity because it helps the student to discover the function of phonics and the way words are put together.

At the beginning, students must practice writing with their attention focused upon meaning rather than the correctness of their spelling. To get children to write frequently and to take risks with written language, encourage and accept "invented" or phonetic spelling. As children work with pocket charts and big books and increase their word recognition, they will self-correct their invented spellings. This is a developmental process that occurs naturally in a print-rich environment where children read and write frequently.

Correct spelling of high-frequency words is learned both through applied practice in reading and writing and through direct spelling instruction. High-frequency words often are not phonetically written and must be internalized through repeated use. (See the previous page for a sample list of words that are frequently used in writing.)

Strategies for teaching spelling include the following:

❖ Use the Try Sheet (page 310) while writing.

❖ Circulate among students as they are writing, calling attention to misspelled words.

❖ Use individual lap chalkboards for teacher-guided lessons. Students say words slowly, becoming aware of how their mouths move, hearing their sounds in sequence, and then recording that sequence on the chalkboard. High-frequency words whose meanings are understood should be practiced using the following strategy:

1. Teacher says the word.

2. Students repeat the word.

3. Teacher uses the word orally in the context of a sentence.

4. Teacher writes the word correctly on the overhead projector or chalkboard.

5. Students copy the word correctly on an individual chalkboard.

6. Students look at the word carefully as the teacher says the word.

Spelling and Phonics (cont.)

7. Students continue looking at the word as they say it.

8. Students trace over each letter with their fingers as they spell the word orally.

9. Students completely erase the chalkboard.

10. Students rewrite the word from memory.

11. Immediately, the teacher spells the word correctly so students can check and correct, if necessary.

Alphabet activities can teach phonics and spelling. Any activity that attaches letters with sounds or entails an analysis of word structure is good practice.

The practice of utilizing word lists for practice and eventual mastery is also a legitimate strategy. Be sure that practice with the spelling/phonics words occurs in some meaningful context before they are practiced in isolation.

These lists can include three types of words. First, use words with similar patterns or phonograms (like *cat, sat, flat,* or *king, ring, wing*). These words are not difficult once the pattern is internalized and generalization to other similar words naturally occurs. Second, include frequently used words that may or may not be phonetically correct. The premise behind this is that these words have been practiced and applied many times before. Last, be sure to include some theme words pertaining to the literature and topics currently being studied. These words may be challenging.

When initially assigning a word list, administer a pre-test to establish which words have already been mastered. Use the First-Try Spelling Test on page 307 for this. Students should correct this pre-test themselves under teacher supervision. This leads to self-motivation and achievement.

Dictation

Dictation sentences are an effective bridge between spelling and daily writing. They should include only spelling words that have been mastered. Before giving the dictation sentence, signal for the children to listen and then recite the whole sentence. The children repeat the whole sentence out loud before they are allowed to write it. The teacher repeats the dictation sentence only once while students are writing. Have the students touch each word as you repeat the words one last time after they have finished writing. Provide a model for the children to use to check their work. This can be written on the chalkboard or overhead projector, or the teacher may have prepared sentence strips to place in the pocket chart. Be sure they understand and check punctuation as well as spelling.

First-Try Spelling Test

	My First Try	Correct Spelling	Need to Practice
1.			
2.			
3.			
4.			
5.			
6.			
7.			
8.			
9.			
10.			
11.			
12.			
13.			
14.			
15.			

Spelling Sheet

Directions: Draw and label two pictures that begin with the letter _____ and two pictures that begin with the letter _____.

_____
uppercase and lowercase letters

_____
uppercase and lowercase letters

Practice the letters.   Print your words.

Spelling Test

Spelling Test

 Spelling Test

Name: _____ Date: _____

Name: _____ Date: _____

_____

_____

_____

_____

_____

_____

_____

_____

_____

_____

_____

_____

_____

_____

_____

Try Sheet

Your Try	Teacher	Write the word again correctly.

My Alphabet Dictionary

Directions: Write a word for each letter.

Aa is for _____	**Bb is for** _____	**Cc is for** _____	**Dd is for** _____
Ee is for _____	**Ff is for** _____	**Gg is for** _____	**Hh is for** _____
Ii is for _____	**Jj is for** _____	**Kk is for** _____	**Ll is for** _____
Mm is for _____	**Nn is for** _____	**Oo is for** _____	**Pp is for** _____
Qq is for _____	**Rr is for** _____	**Ss is for** _____	**Tt is for** _____
Uu is for _____	**Vv is for** _____	**Ww is for** _____	**Xx is for** _____
	Yy is for _____	**Zz is for** _____	

Journal Writing

Journal writing should be used at all grade levels to encourage writing. It is an integral part of the curriculum that gives students freedom to write on whatever topic interests them. Students become more confident and fluent writers as a result of this.

During journal-writing time, it is quite useful for the teacher to circulate throughout the classroom, discussing students' journal entries with them. Comment positively on something that is good, but also cite one thing that can be improved. Be sure that whatever item or skill you are pointing out is at an understandable level to that student. Simply mention a correction, explain the reason why, and encourage the student to correct it.

Later take the time to read what your students have recorded in their journals. Write a brief reply to the student. This reply should be in response to the content.

Use Try Sheets (page 310) with your class. These will cut down on the inevitable question, "How do I spell this word?" Before students write in their journals, have them take out their Try Sheets. As they get to a word they're not sure how to spell, have them write it in the Your Try column. As you circulate around the classroom, look at the Try Sheets and write the word correctly in the Teacher column. If the student has spelled it correctly, put a happy face in this column. The student then copies the word correctly in the last column. Limit them to one or two words a day. In this way they can learn the correct spellings.

Journals are an assessment tool since they give teachers valuable insight into their students' strengths, weaknesses, and interests. They also illustrate growth in a student. For this reason, students should be encouraged to date each entry. At parent conferences, share journals to illustrate students' abilities and progress. You may wish to institute a policy where students are allowed to fold over pages that they do not want to share. Be sure you keep their trust.

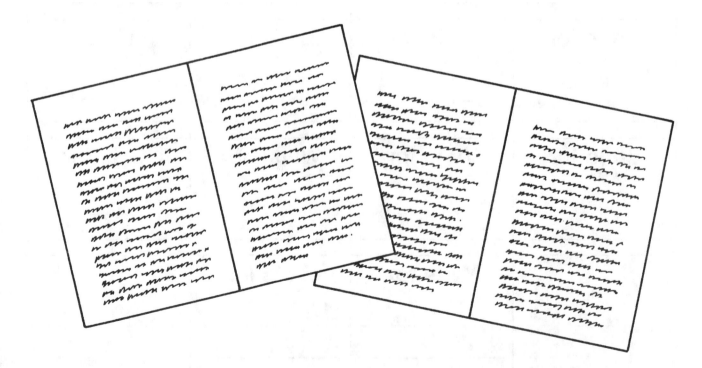

Writing Topics

General	Seasonal
My Birthday	The Scarecrow Who Ran Away
It Was a Dark and Scary Night	The Funniest Costume
Rain, Rain, Go Away	Trick or Treat!
The Day the Ocean Froze	How to Make an Apple Pie (First, you plant an apple seed . . .)
The Day I Was Invisible	Tom Turkey
My Favorite Things	The Family Get-Together
The Happy Day	The Holiday Surprise
The Very Sad Day	Holiday Lights
In the Park	Why Santa Wears Red
My Vacation	The Best Gift of All
When I Grow Up	The Magic Christmas Tree
The Best Dog Ever	The Tiniest Elf
Living in Space	The Day It Snowed and Snowed
The Day I Traveled Through Time	When Father Time Missed the New Year
The Day Night Never Came	When Cupid Fell in Love
If I Were the Teacher	Lucky, the Leprechaun
My Best Friend	Pot o' Gold
Getting in Trouble	The Easter Chicken
The Day I Disappeared	April Fools
How I Learned to Fly	It's Great to Be an American (Canadian, Australian, etc.)
The Camping Trip	My Spring Garden

My Favorite Book

Directions: Write the title and author of your favorite book on one side of the book below. Then draw a picture showing something about the book. When you finish, you will have a chance to tell a partner all about this special book.

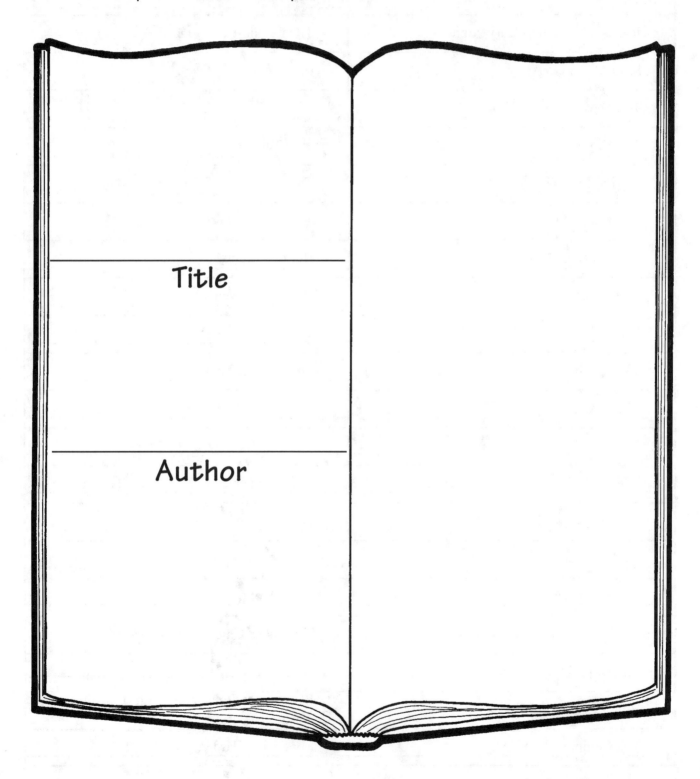

Title

Author

Book Report Form

Title: _____

Author: _____

Time (when the story takes place): _____

Location (where the story takes place): _____

Main characters: _____

_____

What the book is about: _____

_____

_____

_____

What part did you like best? _____

_____

_____

_____

_____

Why? _____

_____

_____

_____

Write two words you learned from this book. Then write what they mean.

1. _____

_____

2. _____

_____

More Book Report Ideas

Book Jacket

Ask the student to design a book jacket for the book. Book jackets normally include the following:

- cover picture showing an important scene, main characters, or theme of the book
- story synopsis
- brief author information
- book review quotes

Character Report

Invite the student to dress as a main character from the book and, using props, tell the class the main events of the book. (**Note:** Videotape these presentations to play during Open House.)

Diorama

Instruct the student to choose one important event from the book. The student should then create a three-dimensional scene of this event in diorama form. A diorama shows depth. The scene can either be created in a box with one full side exposed or in a box with a viewing hole in one side.

Library Poster

Students will enjoy seeing their work on display for the entire school when you ask them to make book posters for the school library. The posters should name the title and author and show an important scene or main character(s) from the book.

Movie Poster

Let the student imagine what the book would be like in movie form. Ask the student to create a movie poster in the same fashion as other movie posters they see on display at the local theater. (Ask a nearby theater for an appropriate sample or two to use as models for your class.)

Oral Language Activities

Primary students arrive in the classroom bursting with something to share. Starting the instructional day by allowing each student to speak to a caring audience sets a supportive, positive tone for learning.

Allow students a few minutes to hang up wraps and unpack bookbags. After students have reported to their seats, promptly start the following activity. At first many students will not be prepared to participate quickly, but eventually all students will participate.

"Snap Clap" Oral-Response Chant

1. The teacher poses a question that will require more than a yes or no answer. (For example: "Are you buying lunch or did you bring it today?")

2. The teacher and the students begin this snap-clap pattern in a rhythm:

① slap (both hands slap lap once)   ② clap (both hands clap once)   ③ snap (right hand); snap (left hand)

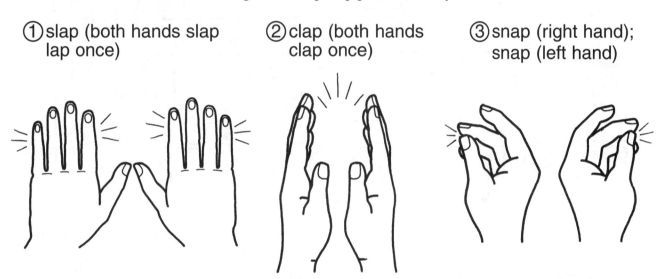

The teacher calls on a specific student while "snap-clapping." (slap; clap; "Su"—snap right hand; "sie"—snap left hand; "Susie")

3. Student responds by answering the question in a complete sentence. ("I brought my lunch to school today.")

4. The teacher immediately restates the child's response, modeling correct grammar if the student has made any errors. ("You brought your lunch to school today.")

5. The teacher follows steps 1–4 calling on each student.

6. Two questions may be asked of the students at the same time, with responses given one after the other. Ask questions that require complete sentence responses.

   If a child has difficulty responding due to language barriers or shyness, the teacher may have to provide an answer for the child to repeat. The child will have another opportunity tomorrow to answer on his or her own. No attention is called to improper grammar or wild comments.

   The entire class snap-clap chant should last about 5–10 minutes. As the year progresses, the chant can go faster and become more complex.

Oral Language Activities *(cont.)*

Calendar

Daily calendar activities are an excellent way to develop oral language as well as numerous math skills. Calendar exercises are best done with the whole class participating in the chanting and singing while one child, who is the calendar leader for the day, does the manipulation. Use a large bulletin board for your calendar display. Be sure it is visible to all students and low enough for a child to use.

Choose from the activities below. Vary them from month to month.

- Display a blank month calendar. Make appropriately shaped cutouts to fit in its squares. (For example, you may wish to use pumpkins and ghosts for October.) Each day gives a different child the opportunity to add a pattern piece and write the day's number on the calendar. Establish a pattern for the cutouts. (For example: ghost, ghost, pumpkin; ghost, ghost, pumpkin.) As the pieces are added each day, the pattern can be recited and the shape of the next day's cutout predicted.

- Display the months of the year in order. Recite or sing these with the leader pointing to appropriate month labels.

- Make and hang labels: Yesterday was; Today is; and Tomorrow will be. Have the calendar leader add the appropriate day of the week after each. Then lead the class in an oral recitation of the completed sentences. The month and numbers can be added to make the sentences more complex.

- Staple the center of a 12" piece of yarn under each day of the week. Have the calendar leader tie a bow under the appropriate day of the week.

- Display a number line from 0–31 for use in counting up to today's date.

- Post a piece of construction paper labeled as the tally sheet. The calendar leader adds a tally mark each day (diagonally slashing each fifth one and circling each group of ten).

- It's fun to keep track of the number of days in school by adding a straw to a container each day. (Many classes work toward a celebration on the 100th day of school!) Model and teach that when 10 ones are together, a bundle or a 10 can be made, and 10 tens make 100.

Oral Language Activities *(cont.)*

Secret Letter Detective

This oral language activity is a guessing game that reinforces letter recognition and phonics, gives responsibility, boosts self-esteem, and engages students in critical thinking and cooperative learning.

Prior to introducing this activity, make the secret letter necklaces and reproduce the parent letter (next page) that accompanies the necklace when it goes home.

Next, decide how often you'd like to incorporate this activity in your schedule (every day, every other day, or once a week). The activity takes about 5–10 minutes to complete, depending on the maturity of the class and the difficulty of the item the detective has chosen. Children will be eager for a turn, so devise a way to manage selection of the detective. Making it one of the classroom jobs is an easy way to accomplish this.

Preparation: When you introduce the secret letter necklace to the class, model how to use it and explain exactly what is expected when it is returned. Each time a child takes home a secret letter necklace, send the accompanying parent letter. Be aware that you may need to take a child aside, help find an item in the classroom, and think of three clues if parent support at home does not exist.

Cut poster board into 3" (8 cm) squares. Punch a hole near the top center. Insert a 3' (90 cm) piece of craft yarn and knot to form the necklace. Write a different letter on each in dark permanent marker. Store them on low hooks so students can choose their own.

Student Directions

1. Take the necklace and note home.

2. Find something that contains that letter's sound.

3. Think of three clues that will help the class guess what it is.

4. Hide the item in a container so that it remains a secret from all members of the class.

5. During oral language activities, stand on a speaking platform:

   - Show and identify the letter to the class.
   - Identify all the sounds that the letter makes in this word and others. The class echoes the sounds.
   - Tell where the sound occurs in the word that names your object—beginning, middle, end.
   - Give the first clue.
   - Watch the second hand on the clock for one minute so that the class has ample time to think.
   - Choose a child by name. Listen to the guess. Tell him or her if it is correct. If is not, chose another classmate to guess. Listen to three guesses before giving another clue.
   - This is repeated until the item is guessed or the detective has given three clues and received three guesses for each clue.
   - If no one can guess, the child remains the secret letter detective for one more day.

Oral Language Activities *(cont.)*

Secret Letter Detective

Date_____

Dear Parents,

Today your child is wearing a Secret Letter Necklace home. Your child is responsible for bringing something to school tomorrow that contains the letter's sound. The item your child chooses must be hidden in a bag, box, etc., because it is a secret! Your child must be prepared to present three clues to the class which will help them guess what it is. Please help your child practice these clues so he or she is prepared to present them orally to the class.

If he or she "stumps" the class (if no one can guess), your child will remain secret letter detective for one more day.

The purposes of this oral language activity are to reinforce letter recognition and phonics, to give responsibility to students which boosts self-esteem, and to engage the entire class in critical and cooperative thinking.

Thanks for your help!

Sincerely,

_____

Oral Language Activities *(cont.)*

Word Walking

Word Walking is a fun activity for use in practicing and reinforcing sight words or vocabulary words. These words must have been taught in context prior to practicing the words in isolation.

Directions:

1. Make a tagboard pattern of the foot below.

2. Trace around the pattern several times on construction paper. Turn the pattern over and trace an equal number of times to make left feet.

3. Cut out the feet.

4. Using a thick marker, write a word on each foot. Use an equal number of left feet and right feet.

5. Cover with clear, adhesive paper on both sides or laminate.

6. To play, instruct students to place footprints on the floor and read the words aloud as they walk over them.

7. As extensions, arrange the words in sentences or have students put them into alphabetical order and walk over them.

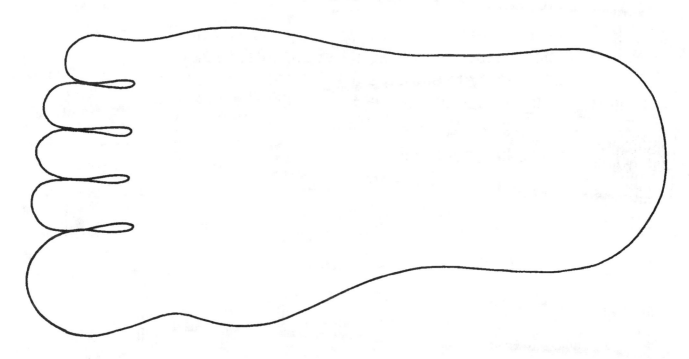

Oral Language Activities (cont.)

Speaking Platform

In a classroom where reading, writing, listening, and speaking are interconnected throughout the instructional day, a speaking area is quite useful. If you are lucky enough to have a small stage, use it. If not, you might decide to make a small platform. Make sure that it is sturdy, steady, and mobile.

There are other ways to make students stand apart from the rest of the class while speaking. The easiest is to acquire a large carpet square (3' x 3' or 1 m x 1 m) or small are a rug. Designate this rug as your "speaker's platform." This can be decorated by adding some fancy braid, trim, or stars. Anytime students speak in front of the class, have them stand on this special "platform." This can easily be moved around the classroom and be stored in a closet.

Acquiring and using a speaking platform will positively affect your students in the following ways:

The sharing of thoughts and writings will increase.

Public speaking skills will improve.

Listening skills will improve.

Students will learn to respect the speaker.

Student-authored stories will become accepted as more authentic.

Students will realize that the teacher is not always the person in control of the class.

Students will be motivated to stand proudly and to share.

Today in History

Name:_____

1. Date today:_____ 2. My historical date:_____

3. What event took place on this date? _____

_____

_____

_____

_____

4. Why was this important? _____

_____

_____

_____

_____

5. Who was involved? _____

_____

_____

_____

_____

6. How does this event affect me today?_____

_____

_____

_____

_____

7. Why I would (or would not) like to have participated in this event:

_____

_____

_____

_____

Mapping

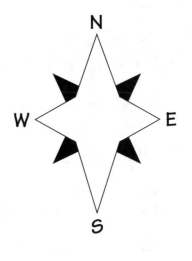

Map Key

The United States

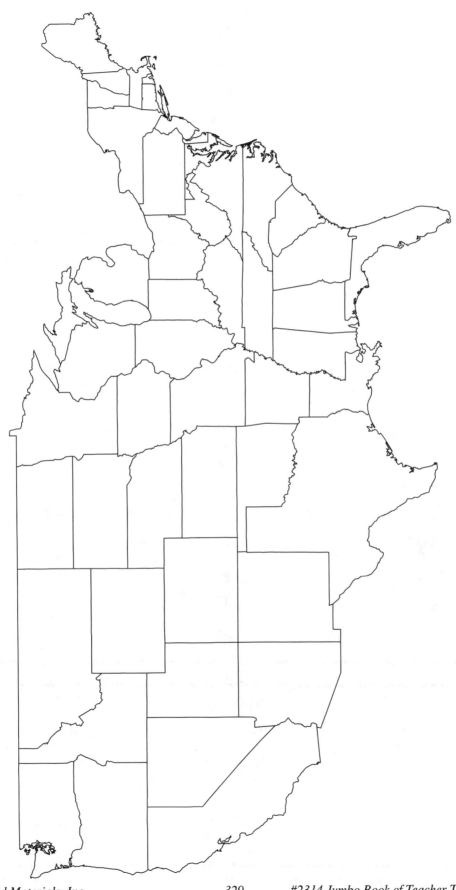

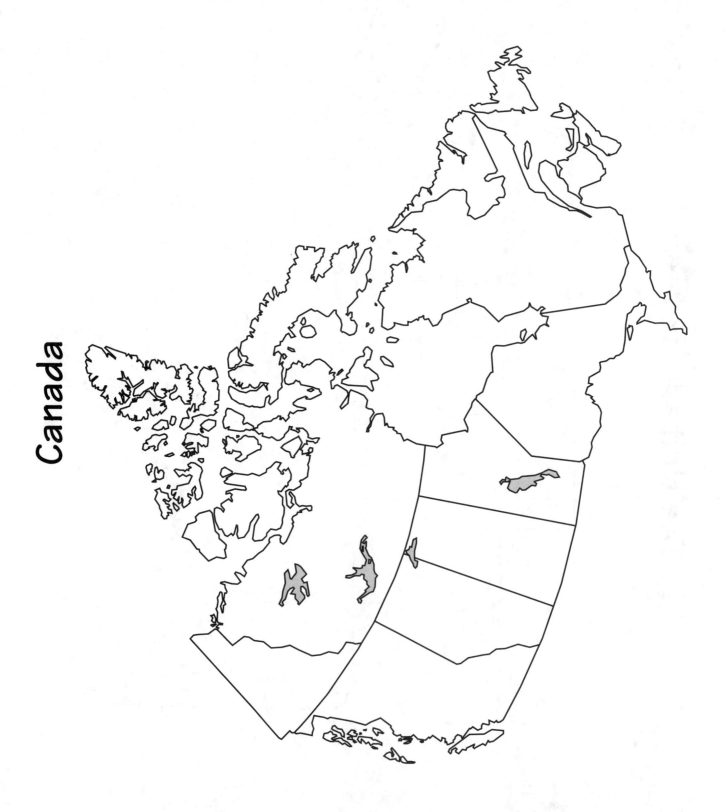

Canada

North America

Europe

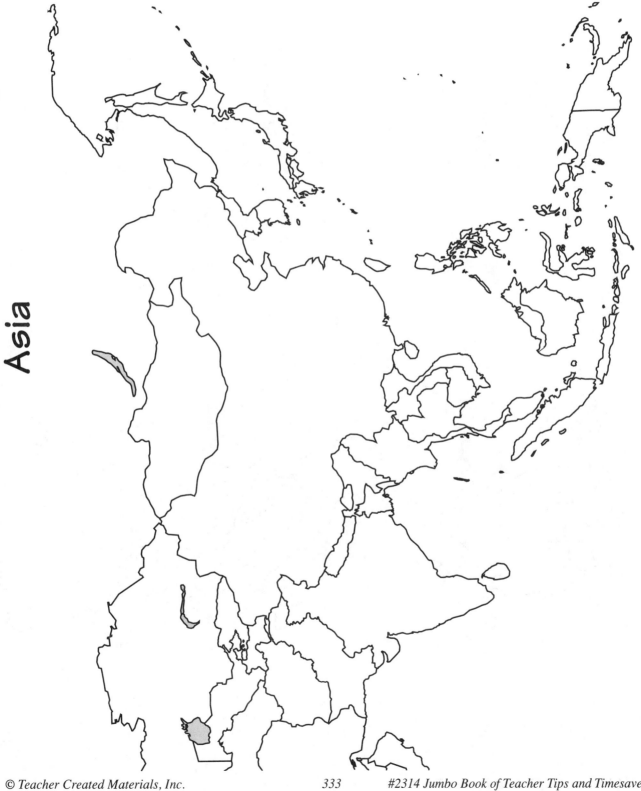

Asia

Australia

Africa

South America

Antarctica

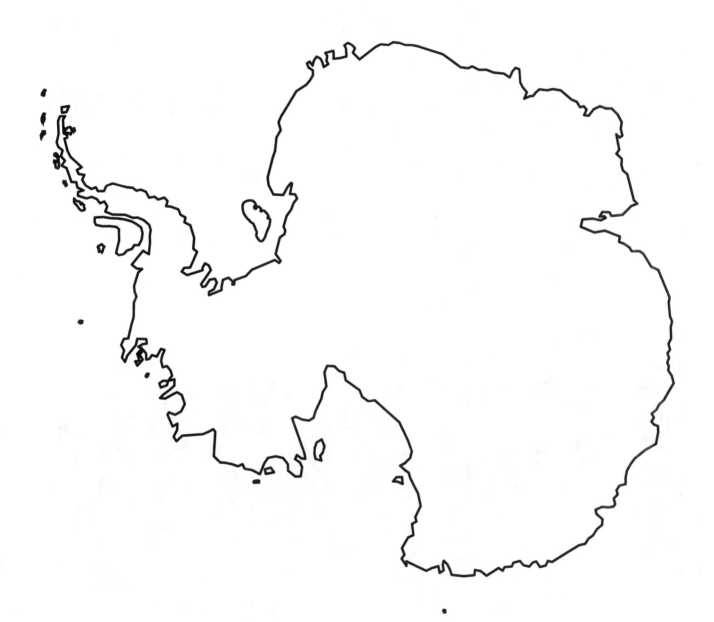

Science Observation Area

Incorporated throughout your units will be many opportunities for real-life science experiments. For example, classroom critters can be learning tools if students are given time and space to observe them and make discoveries about them.

A Science Observation Area should be a part of all classrooms. In setting up your science area, be sure that it is low enough for students to observe without touching or picking up the displays and experiments. Model early the "don't touch" and "please touch" types of behaviors. As children visit this area during center time, expect to hear stimulating conversations and questions among them. Encourage their curiosity, but respect their independence!

Provide Science Observation Journals (see page 339) so students can independently record observations and discoveries. After a time, be sure to be available to assist the class in making conclusions and extending what they have learned in some way.

Books with facts pertinent to the animal, item, or process being observed should be provided for students who are compelled to research more sophisticated information.

Sometimes it is very stimulating to set up a science experiment or add something interesting to the Science Observation Area without a comment from you at all!

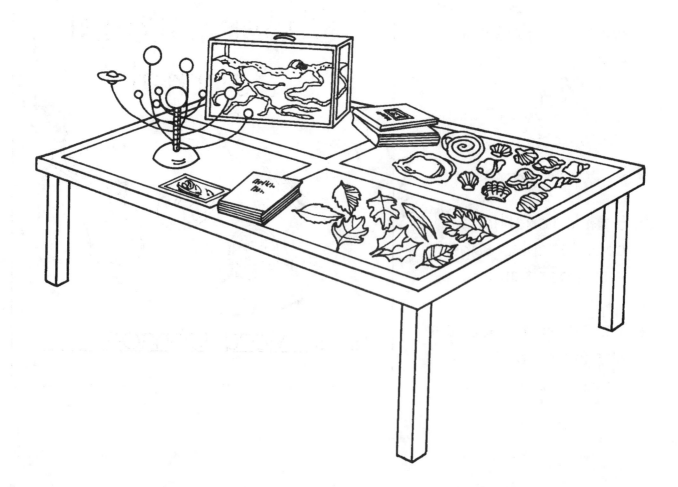

Science Observation Journal

Science Observation Journals are an effective way to integrate science and language arts. Students simply record their observations and thoughts or questions about those observations in a journal kept in the science area. The observations may be recorded with words or sketches which keep track of changes both in the science item or in the thoughts and discussions of the students.

Science Observation Journal entries can be completed as a team effort or an individual activity. Be sure to model making and recording observations several times when introducing the journals to the science area.

Use the student's recordings in the Science Observation Journals as a focus for class science discussions. You should lead these discussions and guide with probing questions, but it is not usually necessary for you to give any explanation. Students come to accurate conclusions as a result of classmates' comments and your questioning.

How to Make a Science Observation Journal

1. Cut two pieces of 8 ½"x 11" (22 cm x 28 cm) construction paper to create a cover.

2. Insert several Science Observation Journal sheets.

3. Staple together and cover stapled edge with book tape.

4. Title it and place it in the Science Observation Area.

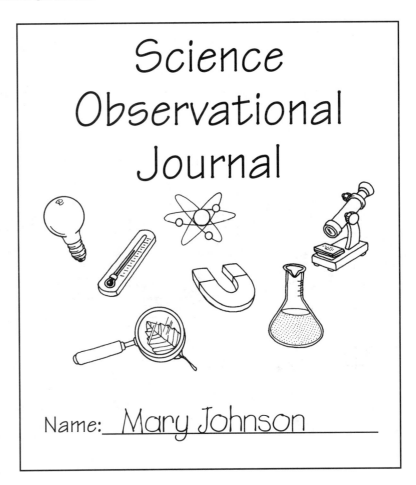

Science Observation Journal Page

Science Observation Journal

Date	What Was Observed	Observer

Science Experiment Form

Name _____ Date _____

My Experiment _____

Question	**What do I want to find out?**

_____
_____

Hypothesis	**What do I think?**

_____
_____

Procedure	**How will I find out? (step by step)**

1. _____
_____

2. _____
_____

3. _____
_____

4. _____
_____

5. _____
_____

Results	**What actually happened?**

_____
_____

Conclusions	**What did I learn?**

_____
_____

Weather Chart

What's the weather like where you live? On the bottom of this page is a weather chart. There are also weather pictures provided on this page. Every day, draw a picture in your chart that shows what the weather is like.

After completing the chart, decide what kind of weather you like best. Draw a picture in the space below to show how you would dress for the weather that day.

Cloudy

Sunny

Rainy

Snowy

Windy

Thundershowers

Sunday	Monday	Tuesday	Wednesday	Thursday	Friday	Saturday

Math

The foundations of a strong mathematics instruction in your classroom should be child-centered and based on discovery learning. For math concepts to be meaningful and thus internalized, the activities must be process-oriented, utilizing thought as well as memorization.

As with learning the system of print in our language, math instruction must have the child at the center of the activity. The effective math teacher stimulates the student to learn by serving as a model and a guide as the child uses math manipulatives and functional, real-life objects to discover our number system. Patterns and order in numbers, relationships among them, and likenesses and differences in mathematical properties are gained through process skills and thinking activities.

Problem solving and logic, which are major parts of the math curriculum, should be modeled and discussed by the teacher with many whole group and/or cooperative group experiences followed by individualized practice and application.

Integrate math concepts and activities with literature. This can be accomplished by making children aware of math concepts as they are found in literature. As you read, point out the uses of numbers, measurement, geometry, and problem solving found in stories. Tell children in advance what math concepts to look for. Talk about these when you have finished reading. Extend this by developing sample problems based on literature.

On the following pages you will find a variety of reproducible pages and manipulative sheets to help with your math program.

Number Sheet

1	2	3	4	5
6	7	8	9	10
11	12	13	14	15
16	17	18	19	20

Hundreds Sheet

1	2	3	4	5	6	7	8	9	10
11	12	13	14	15	16	17	18	19	20
21	22	23	24	25	26	27	28	29	30
31	32	33	34	35	36	37	38	39	40
41	42	43	44	45	46	47	48	49	50
51	52	53	54	55	56	57	58	59	60
61	62	63	64	65	66	67	68	69	70
71	72	73	74	75	76	77	78	79	80
81	82	83	84	85	86	87	88	89	90
91	92	93	94	95	96	97	98	99	100

Times Tables

X	0	1	2	3	4	5	6	7	8	9
0	0	0	0	0	0	0	0	0	0	0
1	0	1	2	3	4	5	6	7	8	9
2	0	2	4	6	8	10	12	14	16	18
3	0	3	6	9	12	15	18	21	24	27
4	0	4	8	12	16	20	24	28	32	36
5	0	5	10	15	20	25	30	35	40	45
6	0	6	12	18	24	30	36	42	48	54
7	0	7	14	21	28	35	42	49	56	63
8	0	8	16	24	32	40	48	56	64	72
9	0	9	18	27	36	45	54	63	72	81

Art

Integrating art with reading, writing, listening, and speaking is a wonderful way to get children motivated and engaged actively in learning language. Analyzing characteristics and details in order to draw requires high-level thinking skills and refined eye-hand coordination. When children choose to use the art center, encourage the addition of labels, words, and/or sentences to the art they create.

In this area you should provide many different supplies and tools with which children can create. Listed below are suggestions:

- crayons
- washable markers
- colored pencils
- scissors
- glue sticks
- stencils (letters and pictures)
- drawing paper
- old magazines

- shapes to trace
- step-by-step art instruction books
- real photographs of items pertaining to your unit of study
- an easel with paints
- construction paper

The Writing Process

The Real Life Approach

The writing process is the "real life" approach to teaching students how to write. It replicates the way people really use writing daily as a life skill and a creative tool.

People who "really" write first have a need to write, either practical or creative. They make notes as ideas occur to them. They may have an intensive private brainstorming session to start their process. Then they look at their notes or brainstormed list. They choose, prioritize, and organize the information and then they put their first draft on paper. If they have time, they may put this draft away for some time in order to take a fresh look at it later. Then they edit. They may ask someone to proof their work and to provide feedback. Only after all this does the "real" writer attempt a final draft. Even this draft may need more revision, perhaps for clarity or for the addition of concrete examples.

Steps in Teaching the Writing Process

Using the writing process in the classroom is an attempt to use steps outlined above to make writing real to students. First, the student is presented with a reason to write. This can be a discussion, a visual experience, a reading selection, and so on. An individual or class brainstorming session follows. Students are then allowed to organize their ideas. They may be comfortable with outlining or clustering. It is nice to give them more than one organizational technique. At this point, the students write their first drafts. They should be encouraged to get their ideas on paper without undue concern for the mechanics of writing.

The editing process follows the first draft and may result in multiple drafts. There can be peer editing, self editing, teacher editing, editing for spelling and mechanics, and/or editing for clarity and style. These parts of the process lend themselves to exercises in cooperative learning and to the use of the computer for word processing. If students are using a computer, they should print each successive draft for optimum practice in tracing the growth of a piece of writing. These successive drafts are ideal for portfolio assessment.

Different from the Traditional Method

This process differs in three notable ways from the traditional method of teaching writing. First, the writing process can stop at any point. The students or the teacher can say, "I've got what I need from this piece. I'll leave it at this point." Second, students are not expected to produce perfect examples of their writing for grading purposes when what they are really doing is producing a first draft essay for which they had no time to prepare. Third, students are encouraged to learn that writing is a process and to be patient with themselves, to stretch their skills, and to take pride in improving their own work.

Steps in the Writing Process

Teacher Note: Duplicate and distribute this form for students or enlarge and display it in your classroom.

Steps in the Writing Process

Prewriting—everything written before a first draft, including brainstorming, clustering, mapping, outlining, and more

Writing—writing the first draft

Peer Editing—proofreading and editing done by a fellow student

Self-Editing—proofreading and editing done by the author

Revision—changing the writing to improve it

Final Draft—a polished piece of writing

Publishing—producing the writing for others to read, possibly including illustrations

Brainstorming

Teacher Note: *Duplicate this form for individual student or small-group use. Display it on an overhead for whole-class brainstorming. The topic should be written on the first line and all supporting or related ideas on the lines beneath.*

- -

Brainstorming

_____

Topic

Ideas

_____ _____

_____ _____

_____ _____

_____ _____

_____ _____

_____ _____

_____ _____

_____ _____

_____ _____

_____ _____

Clustering

Teacher Note: Duplicate this form for individual student or small-group use when gathering brainstormed ideas into a beginning structure. Explain that each topic will need (at least) three supports, and each support needs (at least) three examples or explanations. The central topic is placed where indicated, and each support branches from it. Corresponding information relating to each support is extended from it as indicated.

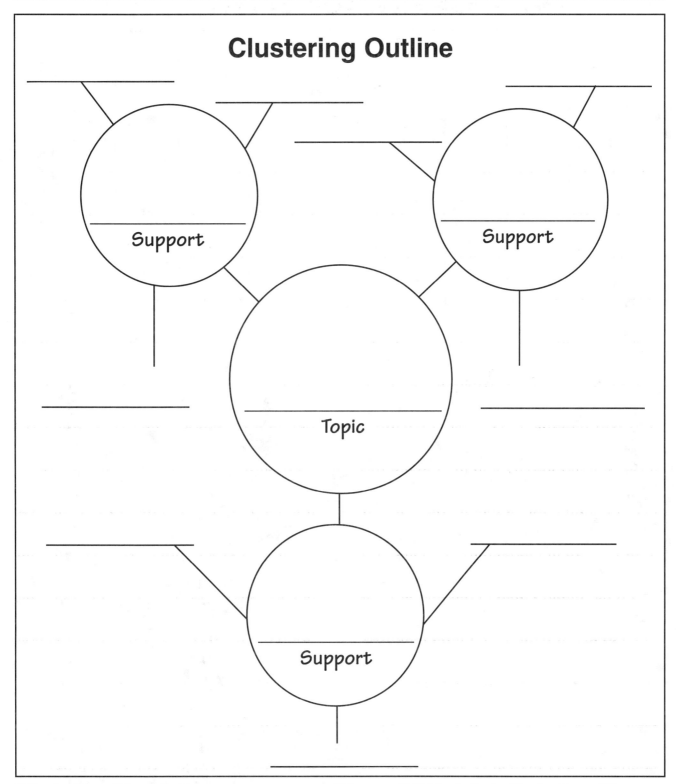

Clustering Outline

Support

Support

Topic

Support

Clustering *(cont.)*

Teacher Note: *This form, like the last one, can be duplicated for individual student or small-group use when gathering brainstormed ideas into a beginning structure. The difference between the two is that this one has a beginning outline structure. Explain that each topic will need (at least) three supports, and each support needs (at least) three examples or explanations. The central topic is placed where indicated, and each support branches from it. Corresponding information relating to each support is extended from it as indicated.*

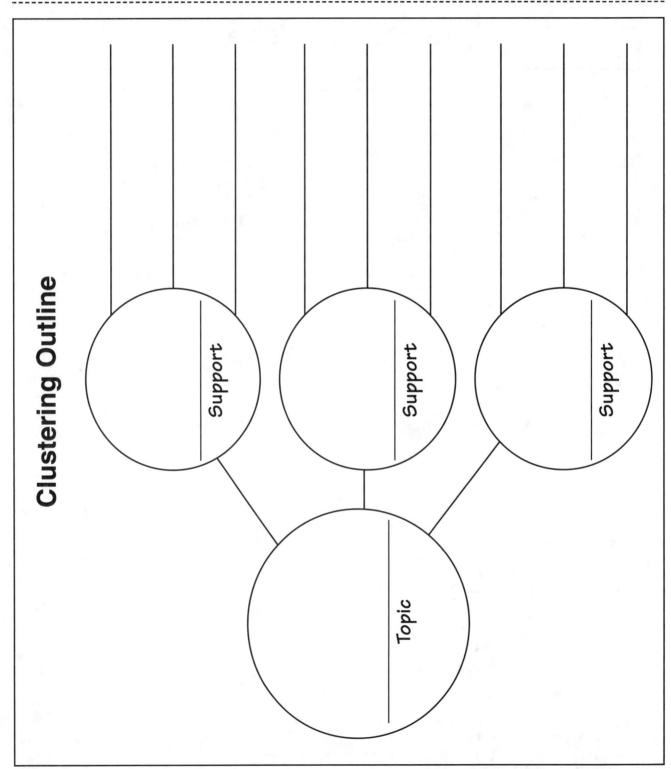

Clustering Outline

Support

Support

Support

Topic

Outlining

Teacher Note: *Duplicate this form for individual student or small-group use when preparing a report or essay. A cluster can be done first and then organized into an outline, or the outline can be made immediately from initial brainstorming. Be sure to model correct outlining before the students work on their own. Several examples done as a class will be especially beneficial. Remember, each of the three supports is stated in the introduction. They become the main ideas of the following three paragraphs and receive their own supports. The introduction is usually recapped in the concluding paragraph.*

Outlining

_____

Topic

I. Introduction:

    A. _____

    B. _____

    C. _____

II. (I. A)

    A. _____

    B. _____

    C. _____

III. (I. B)

    A. _____

    B. _____

    C. _____

IV. (I. C)

    A. _____

    B. _____

    C. _____

V. Conclusion:

    A. _____

    B. _____

    C. _____

Peer-Editing Response I

Peer-Editing Response

The piece I read was _____

by _____.

The best thing about this piece is_____

_____

_____.

It would be even better if _____

_____

_____

_____

_____.

_____   _____
            Peer Editor   *Date*

Peer-Editing Response I *(cont.)*

Teacher Note: This is a sample of the completed form from the previous page.

Peer-Editing Response

The piece I read was _"The Apple Tree"_

by _Ashley Palmire._

The best thing about this piece is _the description of the animals_ _and bugs that live in the tree._

_____

It would be even better if _some of the spelling was checked._

_____

_____

_____

_____

_____Jessica Traxler_____   _____April 16_____
Peer Editor   Date

Peer-Editing Response II *(cont.)*

Teacher Note: This form can be duplicated for use in the middle and upper grades. Students can use it to respond to other students' writing.

Peer-Editing Response

Author: _____

Title: _____

Name three or more things the author does well.

_____

_____

_____

_____

_____

Name two or more things the author can do to improve the writing.

_____

_____

_____

_____

_____

_____   _____
          Peer Editor   *Date*

    356

Peer-Editing Response II *(cont.)*

Teacher Note: *This is a sample of the completed form from the previous page.*

Peer-Editing Response

Author: *Matthew Leewood*

Title: *"Summer Days"*

Name three or more things the author does well.

He describes the feeling of the sun so that I feel like I am there.

The spelling is very good.

The part with the ice cream is funny.

Name two or more things the author can do to improve the writing.

I think some of the sentences are run-ons. (I marked them on the paper.)

I wasn't always sure who was talking. Make that part clearer.

Amy Williams
Peer Editor

March 21
Date

Self-Editing Response I

Teacher Note: This form can be duplicated and used for the primary student to reflect on his or her own writing at the self-editing stage.

SELF-EDITING RESPONSE

Name: _____

Date: _____

Title: _____

What I like best about this writing is _____

_____

_____

_____

_____.

What I need to improve in this writing is_____

_____

_____

_____.

Self-Editing Response I (cont.)

Teacher Note: This is a sample of the completed form from the previous page.

SELF-EDITING RESPONSE

Name: _Marcella Bahkta_

Date: _May 3_

Title: _The Circus Day_

What I like best about this writing is _the part about the_

clown.

What I need to improve in this writing is _to check my spelling._

Self-Editing Response II

Teacher Note: This form can be duplicated and used for the middle and upper elementary student to reflect on his or her own writing at the self-editing stage.

Self-Editing Response

Name: _____

Date: _____

Title: _____

The Best Part: _____

_____

_____

What Needs Improvement: _____

_____

_____

If you did not write this, would you still enjoy reading it?

_____

Compared to other writing you have done, how would you rate this piece?

_____

Do you think this piece should be included in your portfolio?

_____

Self-Editing Response II *(cont.)*

Teacher Note: This is a sample of the completed form from the previous page.

Self-Editing Response

Name: *William Hughes*

Date: *September 30*

Title: *The Giraffe Who Could Fly*

The Best Part: *I really used my imagination to show what it would be like if a giraffe really could fly. I think I made it funny.*

What Needs Improvement: *I need to take a good look at my sentences. I don't think they are all complete.*

If you did not write this, would you still enjoy reading it?

Yes, I would. I'm even curious to see what it is like when it's finished!

Compared to other writing you have done, how would you rate this piece?

This is one of my best writings because it is creative.

Do you think this piece should be included in your portfolio?

I will probably include it.

Publishing

There are many student writings that can be published. Here are a few:

- stories
- poetry
- essays
- reports
- student anthologies
- student newspapers
- autobiographies
- plays and skits

- interviews
- storyboards
- original song lyrics
- jokes
- dialogs
- book, movie, and television reviews
- recipes
- sports statistics

There are also many ways to publish a piece of writing, as well as a variety of things to do with it once it is published. Here is a list of good ideas. As you think of others, add them to this list.

- Bind it into a book.
- Create a class collection, gathering writing from each student into one book.
- Send it to a children's magazine.
- Illustrate it.
- Send it to a community magazine or newspaper.
- Videotape readings of the writing to share with other classes.
- Display it at a Back-to-School Night, Open House, or other family event.
- Exchange finished writings for students to share at home with their families.
- Create a classroom card catalog of student-written books. Keep them in your classroom library.
- Ask students to write book reports on other students' books.
- Write and produce screenplays from original stories.
- Have a poetry reading.

Publishing Company

Publishing student-authored books is highly effective in boosting their confidence as writers. It also makes the writing process relevant in the children's lives; they realize the authors are real people and that they themselves are capable of being authors.

Setting up a publishing company is not difficult, and it can be used continuously with little maintenance. Choose a location in your classroom with a small partition for display of a publishing company sign (a small bulletin board or poster). Be sure the location has ample counter or table space for the following:

❏ a supply of pre-made books for publishing

❏ receptacle(s) for crayons, colored pencils, markers, pastels, and letter stencils or rub-on letters for titles (which are to be used as publishing supplies only)

❏ space to display already published books

❏ space for storage of books as writing references, like dictionaries (at all levels), word books, etc.

Obtain manuscripts (stories) for publishing from journal entries, creative writing assignments, or stories written by individual students during open work time. Be sure that all students at all ability levels periodically publish books.

For less able and English as a second language students, simply take dictation, using the following method, and allow them to illustrate. After the students have selected what to publish, meet with them to print their words in a blank book. As the students read the manuscript to you, repeat and write their ideas, making them grammatically correct while keeping ideas as near to the original words as possible. Write a sentence or two on each page, using a dark pen. Be sure to edit spelling, punctuation, etc., as you rewrite the story with the student watching. Guide the student-author in deciding on an appropriate title for the book which reflects the main idea of the story. Finally, before allowing the student to illustrate the book, have him or her practice reading it to you.

Where to Publish Outside the Classroom

Many magazines and papers publish original student work. Contact the organizations below for details about their current publishing standards and submission requirements.

1. Original writing and art from children ages 8 to 14 can be sent to

> **The Flying Pencil Press**
> P.O. Box 7667
> Elgin, IL 60121

2. Original writing and art from children ages 5 and up can be sent to

> **Cricket League**
> P.O. Box 300
> Peru, IL 61354

3. Original writing and art from students through age 13 can be sent to

> **Stone Soup**
> P.O. Box 83
> Santa Cruz, CA 95063

4. Original stories, articles, and craft ideas and directions can be sent to

> **Highlights for Children**
> 803 Church Street
> Honesdale, PA 18431

5. Original written and illustrated stories can be sent to

> **The National Written & Illustrated By . . . Awards Contest for Children**
> **Landmark Editions, Inc.**
> P.O. Box 4469
> Kansas City, MO 64127

6. Original responses to fiction or nonfiction can be submitted to

> **The Perfection Form Company**
> 1000 North Second Avenue
> Logan, Iowa 51546

Binding Books

Here and on the following page are directions for two bookbinding methods.

Hinged Cover

1. Cut the front and back covers slightly larger than the book's pages.

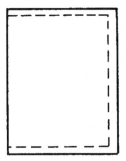

2. Cut a ¼" to ½" (.6 cm to 1.3 cm) strip from the left side of the front cover.

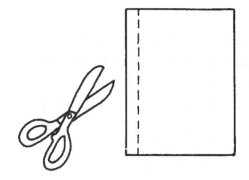

3. Tape the two pieces together again, leaving a narrow opening between the two. Use regular adhesive tape or another very flexible tape.

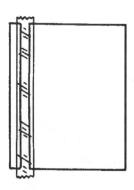

4. Staple or glue the book's pages and cover together.

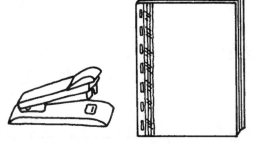

5. Cover the hinge and staples with bookbinding tape wide enough so the hinge and opening do not show.

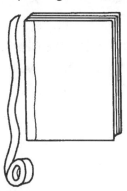

Binding Books (cont.)

Paper- or Cloth-Covered Book

1. Cut two pieces of cardboard or tagboard. They should be slightly larger than the book's pages since they are the front and back covers.

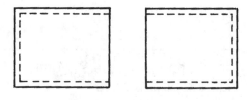

2. Lay the covers next to each other on a piece of cloth or wrapping paper. Leave a small space between them. The cloth or paper should be about 2" to 3" (5 cm to 8 cm) larger around the whole perimeter.

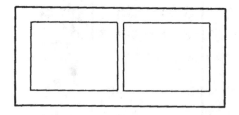

3. Cut the paper or fabric corners so they will fold smoothly.

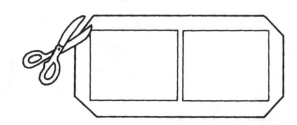

4. Place glue along the four outside edges of the covers. Then fold the cloth over and press it down firmly.

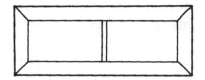

5. Stitch or staple the final written pages together down the center, adding one extra blank sheet to both the front and back.

6. Glue down the blank pages to the inside of the cover. This will cover the fabric or paper opening.

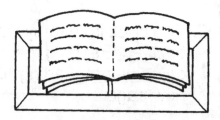

Primary Flip Book

This book is for a specific type of writing. It is particularly useful with beginning writers.

1. With the whole class, brainstorm facts that have been learned on a topic. Record responses, modeling correct usage and spelling and reinforcing vocabulary.

2. Cut 18" x 3" (46 cm x 8 cm) strips of plain paper, four strips per student.

3. Fold the strips in half and place a rubber band around the fold to make a book.

4. Develop a sentence frame with the students that relates to the topic being studied. For example:

   I know that bears

   _____.

5. Write the sentence on the cover.

6. Have the students complete the sentence frame in a different way on each page. For example

       . . . live in the woods.

       . . . are large.

       . . . sleep in the winter.

7. The book is read by flipping back and reading the front cover before reading each new page.

Bibliography

Freeman, Y. and D. *Portfolio Assessment: An Exciting View of What Bilingual Children Can Do.* BEOutreach, January, 1991

Gentry, J. Richard. *Spel Is a Four-Letter Word.* Heinemann, 1987

Hancock, Joelie and Susan Hill, ed. *Literature-Based Reading Programs at Work.* Heinemann, 1988

Kovalik, Susan. *Teachers Make the Difference.* Susan Kovalik and Associates, 1990

McCracken, Robert and Marlene. *A Practical Guide for Primary Teachers.* Peguis, 1979

———. *Reading Is Only the Tiger's Tail.* Peguis, 1972

———. *Stories, Songs, and Poetry to Teach Reading & Writing.* Peguis, 1986

Tierney, R. J., M. A. Carter, and L. E. Desai (eds.). *Portfolio Assessment in the Reading-Writing Classroom.* Christopher-Gordon Publishers, 1991

Trelease, Jim. *The New Read-Aloud Handbook.* Penguin, 1989

Classroom Read-Alouds

Bennett, William J. (ed.). *The Children's Book of Heroes.* Simon & Schuster, 1997

dePaola, Tomie (ed.). *Tomie dePaola's Favorite Nursery Tales.* G. P. Putnam's Sons, 1986

———. *Tomie dePaola's Mother Goose.* G. P. Putnam's Sons, 1985

Dunning, Stephen, et. al. (eds.). *Reflections on a Gift of a Watermelon Pickle . . . and Other Modern Verse.* Scott, Foresman and Company, 1966

Felleman, Haze (ed.). *The Best Loved Poems of the American People.* Doubleday, 1936

Milne, A. A. *The World of Pooh.* E. P. Dutton & Company, 1957

O'Neill, Mary. *Hailstones and Halibut Bones.* Doubleday, 1973

Potter, Beatrix. *The Complete Tales of Beatrix Potter.* Penguin, 1989

Prelutsky, Jack (ed.). *The Random House Book of Poetry for Children.* Random House, 1983

Price, M. (ed.). *A Children's Treasury of Mythology.* Barnes & Noble, 1994

Scarry, Richard. *Richard Scarry's Best Story Book Ever.* Western Publishing Company, 1968

Shnek de Regniers, Beatrice (ed.). *Sing a Song of Popcorn.* Scholastic, 1988

Silverstein, Shel. *A Light in the Attic.* Harper, 1981

———. *Where the Sidewalk Ends.* Harper, 1974

Viorst, Judith. *If I Were in Charge of the World.* Atheneum, 1984